Opening the Heart
of Compassion

M000204902

Opening The Heart of Compassion

Transform Suffering through Buddhist Psychology and Practice

*by Martin Lowenthal
and Lar Short*

Illustrated by Eli Goodwin

Published in the United States by
Martin Lowenthal and Lar Short
Printed by BookSurge LLC, an Amazon.com company

Originally published by Charles E. Tuttle Company in 1993.

The following publishers have generously given permission to use
extended quotes from copyrighted works: From *Wisdom and Compassion: The
Sacred Art of Tibet*, by Marilyn Rhie and Robert Thurman. Reprinted by
permission of Harry N. Abrams, Inc. From *Vital Lies, Simple Truths*, by
Daniel Goleman, Ph.D. Copyright 1985. Reprinted by permission of Simon
& Schuster. From *How to Meditate*, by Kathleen McDonald. Copyright 1984.
Reprinted by permission of Wisdom Publications, Boston. From *Song of the
Profound View*, by Geshe Rabten. Copyright 1989. Reprinted by permission
of Wisdom Publications, Boston. From *Foundation of Tibetan Mysticism*, by
Lama Anagarika Govinda. Copyright 1960. Reprinted by permission of
Samuel Weiser, Inc. From *Cutting Through Spiritual Materialism*, by
Chogyam Trungpa. Copyright 1973. Reprinted by permission of Shambhala
Publications, Inc., Boston. From *Compassion and the Individual* by Tenzin
Gyatso, Copyright 1991. Reprinted by permission of Wisdom Publications,
Boston.

Library of Congress Catalog Card Number: 92-75455

ISBN 1 4196 5133 1

Cover design by Maya Wallach

Text Illustrations © 1993 Eli Goodwin

Acknowledgments

THERE WERE MANY PEOPLE who directly and indirectly assisted in the development and completion of this book. His Holiness Dilgo Khyentse Rinpoche was a source of encouragement for the project of writing about the Heart of Compassion.

We also want to thank the hundreds of students and counseling clients we have worked with who let us into their inner worlds and showed us not only their pains, but their courage and their determination to grow, to be free, and to share the fruits of their spiritual journey.

We are grateful to the members of the Grace Essence Fellowship (GEF) for their support and encouragement. The Dedicated Life Institute and GEF are organizational vehicles for presenting these teachings and for students to support their spiritual growth together.

Special thanks go to Paul Patterson whose suggestions and editing assisted us greatly with the final draft and who contributed the drawing for the meditation in Chapter 10. Joel Friedlander made helpful and wise contributions to the editing and revisions of the entire book. Lastly, but not least, we are grateful for the support, encouragement, and editorial comments of Karen Edwards, Paige Short, Ellen Galford, Micah Lowenthal, and Kevin Lowenthal.

Preface

OPENING THE HEART OF COMPASSION grew out of the authors' collaboration in teaching retreats on the Heart of Compassion, which included meditation practices associated with the Bodhisattva of Compassion. In our intensive eight-day retreats, as well as in writing this book, we integrate our experience and understanding of the conditions of modern life, the timeless issues of pain and suffering, the insights of western psychology, and the lineages of Buddhist philosophy, psychology, and spiritual practice. Our hope is that the result provides a path for understanding ourselves, for the development of wisdom, for the experience of aliveness and growth, and for the realization of true freedom.

We have chosen to offer this amalgam of east and west, of modern and traditional, and of the ordinary and the sacred through teachings about the habits of mind that shape our experience of ourselves and of the world, and which often result in our living in a world of pain. The path out of that suffering to freedom involves taking creative action that is guided by compassion. This compassion is developed through reflection upon the nature of our condition, and insight into our ways of operating as the source of possibilities for suffering or creative expression. To bring us to freedom this compassion has to awaken the aspiration necessary to consciously work with diligence and commitment to operating from a new view. We offer a path for growth beyond our painfully constricted realities. This path uses our own experience and our instinctive concern for others.

The topics that appear in this book are based on universal difficulties and struggles which are typical of our daily life experiences. Reading this book can be an inquiry into the human condition and the human design with the goal of using that design to outgrow the fixations and frames of normal conditions.

There are many ways of describing human fixations, including the systems of Jung, Freud, Rank, Gurdjieff, and Maslow. Some emphasize neurosis, others values, and still others particular neurotic patterns such as guilt or shame. The approach we present here is derived from the Buddhist tradition. It emphasizes (1) the tendency to distort natural impulses of aliveness which are neither good nor bad, (2) our inclination to elaborate these distortions into personal versions of reality and patterns of behavior, and (3) our capacity to use awareness and action to awaken to our natural ways of being, becoming, and acting. We can then use our wisdom qualities and energies to reorganize the way we operate in our daily lives.

We draw on a Buddhist framework because it is oriented towards dealing with everyday life situations and inner processes. This is a handbook on ways of understanding our processes of thinking, feeling, and acting. It gives practices to utilize our capacities for growth. It shows ways of living in a more awakened state of mind day to day and in relationship to others. We are writing, not as Buddhists, but as human beings committed to respecting other people as human beings, and to sharing what we have found to be of value for growth.

The first step in tapping the capacity for awareness is to create a pause in our everyday life and reflect on where we are at this time. This book is designed to assist in that process of aware reflection.

In Part I, the first three chapters, we present a basic introduction. The first chapter deals with the goal of inner freedom and the nature of compassion. Compassion is not only a product of spiritual work, but a practice which can free us from habitual patterns of pain. The second explores the nature of suffering - how suffering arises, the patterns of preoccupation which form the realms of suffering, and how these provide the foundations for growth, wisdom, and freedom. In the third chapter we present the myth of the Great Compassionate One, Avalokiteshvara, as a way to metaphorically introduce the subject of compassion and the worlds of pain, and as a link to the tradition from which the teachings in this book flow.

These discussions are followed in Part II by descriptions of the realms of fixation - the habitual patterns of thinking, feeling and behaving which create suffering - and their underlying dynamics of aliveness. Each realm and dynamic is elaborated in terms of:

1. the principle preoccupations of the realm,
2. what is desired, avoided, and ignored,
3. the postures of the heart in the realm,
4. the double-binds (thought and/or behavior patterns which are contradictory or mutually defeating), wounds, and addictions of the realm,
5. how the realm masquerades as spiritual work,
6. the characteristics of the underlying dynamic of aliveness,
7. the wisdom qualities associated with the dynamic, and
8. meditation practices and inquiries which reveal the dynamic and which develop the wisdom qualities.

The meditations suggested in this book are intended to deepen understanding and to develop the capacity to operate with clarity and aliveness in our everyday lives. Compassion is both a path of consciously working with the energy and awareness of the heart and the fruit of the wisdom that arises from that work.

Part III presents a more comprehensive meditation for developing the energies of the heart center and realizing compassion as a radiant aspect of aliveness. The book concludes with a chapter on the awakening of aliveness and freedom.

Our hope is that this book will contribute to making the nature and depth of perspective of the Buddhist tradition more accessible to those interested in developing their aliveness, their basic nature, and their ability to relate to and share in the world. To the degree that this is possible, may it also serve in some way, however small, to carry the non-sectarian blessing of His Holiness Dilgo Khyentse, Rinpoche to the peoples of the world. In His encouragement to us for this project he wrote:

> This noble work of yours will no doubt contribute a lot in understanding of the Dharma by all interested people not only in the west but also in the east where good books on the subject are still rare. May I wish you all success in your work.

> With my Blessings,
> Yours in the Dharma,
> Dilgo Khyentse Rinpoche

VEN DILGO
KHYENTSE RINPOCHE

SHECHEN TENNYI
DARGYE LING

Table Of Contents

PART I

The Heart of Suffering and Compassion

1

Born to Be Free

An Introduction

We have here the very same breeze as the remote
    spring at Lumbini,
    the birthplace of the Buddha.
The very same mist hangs over the evening garden
    as it did over the
    ancient woods of Asoka trees.
There is no spot on this good earth which is not the
    birthplace
    of a Buddha.

Senzaki Roshi

If anyone strikes my heart, it does not break, but it
bursts. And the flame coming out of it becomes a
torch on my path.

Hazrat Inayat Kahn

LIFE IS A VIBRANT PLAY of energies and opportunities
that we can experience with openness, clarity, joy, and
wonder. The freedom simply to be who we are—to experience
our aliveness, to act with authenticity, to realize the nature of
our being beyond the physical inevitability of death, and to feel

love, connection, and belonging to other people and to the world—is the inspiration, the goal and the birth right of every human being.

Yet we struggle with pain. We long for permanence in a ceaselessly changing world. We desperately seek love, peak experiences, and altered states in our desire to overcome a sense of loneliness and separation. In our lives there is more suffering than freedom, more tension than harmony, more pretense than authenticity, and more numbness than aliveness. Some of us enjoy prosperity and great political, economic, and social freedom. As a society, we possess the expertise to extend that prosperity and freedom to all inhabitants of this planet. Yet we are all uneasy and insecure.

We divide the world into those things we perceive as threatening and those we perceive as supportive. We want relief from the struggle of daily life, we want to know what is going to happen in life, and we are afraid to die. We search for answers that will free us from our prison of suffering and uncertainty, and help us to live each day with simple authenticity.

This book, while not providing the answers that must come from within, offers ideas, teachings, and practices that can help free us from our desire to be "somebody," our urge to prove something, and our fear of living. It presents a working model of compassion that encourages us to engage our thoughts and feelings, discover our underlying dynamics of aliveness, develop our spiritual energies, and nurture the emergence of wisdom.

Buddha and the Path of Everyday Life

There are many religious and philosophical approaches to help us navigate the pains and difficulties of life and work on our spiritual growth. Each school represents a different temperament and level of understanding. The Buddhist tradition in particular provides us with a number of useful guides. First, there is the example of the Buddha. Leaving a materially comfortable and powerful life as a prince, he set out to find the truth about suffering and the cycle of birth and death. Using the tools of his mind and body, he explored his own nature and discovered how to become spiritually free. His enlightenment showed that everybody has the opportunity to attain this state.

Second, this tradition includes a system of psychology and spiritual practice developed over thousands of years. Buddhism places great importance on working with the way we think about and deal with everyday life situations. Tibetan forms of Buddhism, like other tantric traditions, extend the technology of awakening with methods that transform our experiences and our emotions into creative energies that nourish our spiritual growth. This leads to the most exalted states of awareness.

Buddhism is a scientific approach to spiritual work. The teachings of the Buddha emphasize critical self-awareness. We are advised to verify all teachings and spiritual propositions through our own experience and observation. Buddha said:

> Do not believe in anything simply because you have heard it. Do not believe in traditions because they have been handed down for many generations. Do not believe in anything simply because it is found in your religious books. Do not believe in anything merely on the authority of your teachers and elders. But after observation and analysis, when you find that anything agrees with reason and is conducive to the good and benefit of all, then accept it and live up to it.

In Buddhism, understanding as an intellectual exercise is useless unless it also transforms our life. Truth is not something to be learned but a recognition of the nature of reality, which is experienced in all aspects of our being, from the cells in our body to the furthest reaches of our imagination. From this point of view, suffering exists because we are conditioned by ignorance, fear, and neediness. Based on this conditioning we habitually struggle with the world, seeking the freedom to be ourselves. We think that relief lies outside ourselves and must be extracted from the world.

Robert Thurman summarizes the Buddhist path in the following way:

> We may break the cycle by cultivating critical wisdom through investigation of the reality of self and universe. We may systematically overcome ignorance by seeing through the illusion of being a separate "self" and of the universe being an objective other. We realize that everything is free of any intrinsic status, there is no real self to be trapped, no real universe that traps, and also no real off-world isolated state of freedom. Free of the "self" delusion, we become free of self-concern. Free of self-concern, we become free to interact unselfishly with others. Free to interact unselfishly, we no longer experience interaction as suffering; we become able to experience all things happily.

In this book, drawing from Buddhism as an inspiration, we explore the ways in which our thoughts and feelings become fixated as emotional preoccupations. We present a method for developing compassion as a path out of the suffering of those fixations, leading to growth and fearless aliveness.

A Moment of Reflection

Before reading further, you might sit quietly and take a moment to reflect on what it would be like for you to be without self-concern as you go through the activities of your day. What if you were free from thoughts about the past, the future, your needs, and your self-image as you interacted with family, friends, people at work, and strangers? How would this feel now and over time? What sensations in your body would you be aware of? How would you be looking at yourself and the world?

Close your reflection by allowing all thoughts on these questions to dissolve into the space around you, feeling your own desire to become free and happy.

Why Compassion

Compassion is a vital element in releasing the grip of self-concern. When we sense our own longing for freedom and happiness, we realize that others are seeking the same goals. We see that their struggle is similar to our own attempts at growth and satisfaction, and we feel the common bond of our humanity. The awareness of our common desires and struggles and the energy of our bonding to other people nurtures our own spiritual development.

"Opening the Heart of Compassion" refers both to opening the energy and awareness center at the heart and to uncovering the nature of compassion. By concentrating on the heart center (located in the center of the chest), we are able to relate more naturally to ourselves and to others. Working consciously with the energy and awareness in this center overcomes our sense of being stuck and needy, and opens us to feelings of wholeness, love, and belonging.

This process also unlocks the essence of compassion. Compassion does not mean pity or sympathy for the suffering of others, nor does it mean feeling their suffering as our own. When we have compassion, we care for other people with the heartfelt desire to bring about their happiness by freeing them from their own suffering. We take in the pain of others, with the understanding that their suffering arises out of fear, desire, and ignorance. We can do this openly when we have worked through our illusions and fixations in such a way that the essential nature and energy of aliveness, which sought expression in the forms of suffering, is freed from the constrictions of our own habits.

Compassion is not only the result of insight and realization—it is itself a path to freedom. Compassion is the natural and spontaneous response of an open heart. In addition, we are more resourceful and insightful when helping others than when we are concerned solely with ourselves. Compassion—the concern for the well-being and happiness of others—can lead us out of our separate worlds of pain to discover the root causes of all suffering.

The wisdom of compassion—the insight into our nature and into the basic confusion of suffering—comes from opening ourselves wholeheartedly to the unknown and developing the unshakable knowledge of our freedom. The essential nature of compassion is developed as we cultivate the equanimity that can embrace all experiences and all human beings. Compassion is a foundation for sharing our aliveness and building a more humane world.

Beginning with Motivation

The cultivation of compassion begins with two motivations. The first is a compassionate wish to alleviate the suffering of oneself, others, and the world. The second is the desire to see reality clearly, to observe how phenomena arise, and to know how to manifest our essential nature. We all possess the potential to be compassionate in this limitless way and to awaken this potential in others.

Our lives change when we understand that nothing more is needed and that "showing up" is a contribution to the process of life. Consider for a moment that your birth was a demonstration of life contributing to itself through you as you, and that this very world, at this very time, is where you belong.

Your actions can be realized as participation. Ask yourself what the nature and effect of your participation is.

We are the environment that others experience. We can decide to give purpose to the ways in which we show up.

Spiritual Practice

Spiritual practices are designed to help us relax into our natural state and realize our radiance. Through spiritual work we can recognize this radiance in all beings, develop the capacity to surrender to the unknown, accept the unknowable, and consciously develop our physical and energetic capacities. Our aim is to manifest a compassionate, wise, and skillful presence by opening and repatterning our mental and physical habits.

Mind

The mind is more than the thoughts we entertain and the mental capacities we use. At the heart of these phenomena is a vital energy that openly and actively attends to every moment. We need to transcend our ordinary mind of preoccupations and vanities to uncover this subtler, freer mind that has been obscured. Mind, in a spiritual sense, is awareness, a non-physical form of energy. It is inherently clear and reflects everything we experience, like a mirror reflecting everything that passes before it. And just as a mirror remains undisturbed and unaffected by the changing images, no matter how dramatic or intense the event being reflected, so, too, the mind. Unlike the brain, which has thoughts and sensations, the mind is not a thing, but is the space within which all thoughts, sensations, feelings, perceptions, memories, and dreams arise. Mind includes conscious and unconscious experiences, and is the awareness aspect of all phenomena which hosts our experience.

Mind is like the ocean. Just as waves on the surface of the ocean appear agitated while the depths are calm and vast, so, too, the thoughts, emotions, and experiences that make up the turbulent surface of the mind obscure its essentially still and clear nature. We want to experience this stillness and clarity, and be free from our preoccupation with the surface of our oceanic minds. We start to develop these qualities with a pause in our mental and emotional routines. Then, by applying the methods of meditation, we learn how to dive below our everyday bobbing and drifting and enter the deeper qualities underlying our emotions.

To discover and experience these qualities we do not need to become someone or something else. By being human and having the range of human experiences, we qualify.

The mind, not being a thing, is essentially empty. "Empty" does not mean containing nothing, but rather refers to the qualities of openness and spaciousness within which all things arise.

View

When we approach meditation and the unfolding of our universe of habitual thinking, feeling, and acting, it is helpful to develop a close friendship with ourselves and our experience. This friendship is not based on sympathy for stories of our past or hopes for a better future. It grows out of our direct experience of the sensation and energy of each moment. This generates a sense of peace and enjoyment that enables us to embrace all of our experience.

One barrier to this friendly relationship is our conditioned orientation that life is inherently problematic. This attitude reflects our deep longing to overcome our feeling of separation and dis-ease. The way out of these feelings is not the loss of individual consciousness, nor the resolution of all past experiences, nor the dissolution into a cosmic sea. Rather, we can learn to see all things as complete in this very moment.

To understand this view, we may consider incomplete space. Can such a phenomena be conceived? Try to consider, in terms of the physical world, a faulty proton. Try to imagine a defective electron, atom, or molecule. Do such things even make sense? We can only view them as incomplete or defective if we project some idea of how we would like them to be different. Protons, electrons, atoms, and molecules simply are what they are in the form or process that they are in. Physically, we are composed of space and atomic particles. This is true of the physical world, of ourselves, and of others. Their space and particles are no different than ours and ours are no different than theirs.

We simply are "who we are," no matter what we think or feel about it, or what our experiences have been, or what others may think or say. Our presence in the world is the expression in each moment of our being. This is neither good nor bad, flawless nor flawed. It is simply what is.

When we look at everything as just being what it is, we can relate to our experience like a mountain. A mountain simply is. It needs no validation, and requires no changes. In this way, our friendship with experience becomes unconditional, and whatever happens serves to embody aliveness and fullness.

We can relax into a more natural state *at this very moment* and sense it as fresh, vivid, and unspoiled. Nothing is needed and nothing needs to be taken away. Even the weight of our confusion and pain can become light when we penetrate the shield of our hopes and fears and reach the energy of our direct experience. The awareness in this moment is open, luminous and whole rather than clouded by expectation, shaded by disappointment and fragmented by resistance.

Meditation

One goal of meditation is to abide in our nature as a welcoming, hosting presence that effortlessly radiates the Essence qualities of wholeness, and that also helps others recognize this welcoming presence in themselves. To do this we open our hearts to all beings and allow love and compassion to flow to everyone, without limitation or consideration.

Taming the mind and training it to serve the living moment in an open, joyful way is no easy task. ("Moment" does not refer to a unit of time but to an aspect of awareness.) The practice of meditation works with the entire range of our experiences, from the most intense such as anger, panic, and desire, to the quietest and subtlest as in moments of serenity. It includes intellectual processes, emotions, memories, dreams, body sensations, and energies.

Meditation requires that we initially *pause*, interrupting the flow of habitual thinking, feeling and acting. We steadily *open* to the unknown, *reflect* on the machinations of the mind and the nature of reality, *incorporate* and channel the awareness and energy we awaken in the process, and finally *radiate* the results of our efforts.

The aim of meditation is to awaken our aliveness, use it for the direct and intuitive experience of reality, moment to moment, and radiate this in the world. This is called "enlightened presence."

Meditation practices take many forms. One form uses one part of the mind to observe, analyze, and work with the rest of the mind; others involve concentrating on an object or on movements of the body; and some focus on understanding a personal problem and striving to penetrate its origin and nature. Other forms involve the visualization of beings, objects and places that awaken and stimulate qualities within us, and still others communicate with some inner wisdom of our body and mind.

The Tibetan term for meditation, "sgom," literally means "to become familiar." The word "familiar" means "to make like family." The various meditation techniques bring us into a friendly relationship with our own mind, with others, and with the world. Being present and being familiar is a state of mind. While it may be easiest to experience a sense of presence and belonging while sitting quietly in a serene place, this state of mind can be incorporated into every activity and situation, such as working, walking, cooking, eating, listening, and sleeping. In addition to the lifelong cultivation of growth and awakened activity, we realize many short-term benefits. We are less mired in old patterns and become more relaxed. As we release constrictive self-images, we develop an easier and more positive relationship with ourselves. We learn to experience the world more directly and thereby discover more of its richness.

Inner Smiling from the Heart Center

One simple meditation that develops this friendly relationship to ourselves is the *Inner Smile* exercise using the Heart Center. In this meditation, we spread radiant energy by shifting our attention from one part of our body to another, creating a flow of sensation through the body. At the same time, we also get in touch with our aspirations and intentions for our meditation practice—with our "aim." Our aim gives our efforts a direction and aligns our resources with our aspirations.

1. Begin the meditation by placing your attention on your palm or your breath, letting your body and mind ease into the process until you feel relaxed and alert. Now move the attention to the Heart Center.

2. In the Heart Center feel your desire, *during this very meditation*, to become free in the immediate moment—NOW!—building the stamina to abide in the state of poise for the benefit of self and others. Get in touch with any additional aim(s) you have for your practice, feeling the intensity of your intention.

3. Invite the Divine, your teacher, other teachers, deities, supportive forces, and the unknown into your Heart

Center, feeling the increasing radiance of their presence.

4. Spread the radiance from your heart throughout your body like an inner smile. This is like sunbathing from the inside out, with your radiant aim residing like the sun in your heart.

   a. Beginning with your forehead and the top of your head, feel the sensation of radiant **aim** energy flowing throughout your upper head and each area of your brain.

   b. Spread the radiant **aim** energy to the outer edges of your eyes.

   c. Continue to spread the radiant **aim** energy into your nose, through your cheeks and out to your ears.

   d. Spread the radiant **aim** energy to your tongue, mouth, and jaw.

   e. Then to your throat, neck, and chest, including your thymus gland and your lungs.

   f. Fill your liver, adrenals, kidneys with the radiant **aim** energy.

   g. Spread the radiant **aim** energy into all the organs of your abdominal cavity including the stomach, intestines, spleen, pancreas, and sexual organs.

   h. Spread the radiant **aim** energy to your entire body so that your whole body is feeling and radiating the inner smile—every organ, every muscle, every bone, every nerve, and every cell.

2

Seeking Enlightenment Through the Six Realms of Suffering

The range of what we think and do
is limited by what we fail to notice.
And because we fail to notice
that we fail to notice
there is little we can do
to change
until we notice
how failing to notice
shapes our thoughts and deeds.
                    Daniel Goleman, Vital Lies, Simple Truths

Ultimately, the reason why love and compassion
bring the greatest happiness is simply that our nature cherishes them above all else.
                    Tenzin Gyatso, the Fourteenth Dalai Lama

WHEN WE LAUGH at our own follies, when we feel alive with excitement at a circus, or when we are absorbed in the beauty of a sunset, we can realize our own capacity to overcome suffering. In those experiences, we access our basic goodness, our natural radiance, and our potential for happiness. The freedom of humor, the radiance of excitement, and the bliss of absorption are natural to us and can be developed through conscious work. We do not need to be repaired; we do not need to be saved; and we do not need to earn enlightenment. We are not born in sin, hopelessly condemned in this life, or in some way defective. The potential for enlightenment and freedom from suffering is built into us, yet it requires that we explore, nurture, and work with our own awareness and energies.

Designed for Growth

Our human design contains the inherent capacities of our mind and body, as well as our instincts to grow, connect, and make meaning. It also contains capacities that only emerge after we have reached certain stages of growth. Knowing how to reach those stages and develop growth-producing qualities is a key to our freedom. Just as an acorn contains within it the design for the oak tree, so we contain all the ingredients necessary to reach spiritual maturity. However, unless it receives the right nourishment and good soil in which to take root and to grow, the acorn may become squirrel food rather than an oak. Its strength will develop as much from the tests of its environment as from the richness of its soil.

Our spirit grows in the soil of our conscious experiences, extracting nutrients from the energies and insights of those experiences. The ability to extract these nutrients requires taming the mind and reworking the emotional reactions in our bodies. As we develop the wisdom to see through our self-concerns we create the conditions for expressing our happiness. Developing the openness to engage others, we create the sense of belonging. By living life instead of fixing it, we experience life as the precious gift that it is.

The world does not then suddenly change and give us special care and attention or a heavenly reward. Rather, we develop the sense of Grace, a kind of gratitude for the forces that operate in us and in all beings and phenomena.

Choosing Between Struggle and Radiance

Throughout this process, we receive glimpses and then a fuller realization of the fundamental radiance that we already are and always have been. Then our realizations and struggles form the base for developing compassion. Compassion as an experience, a quality of being, and a way of relating to others is also part of the human design. The potential for compassion is developed and matured through the process of living, struggling, and thereby expanding awareness. Through our own experiences, we can know something about human experience. As compassion develops, so does our sense of bonding to other people and to humanity. Our capacity to relate wholeheartedly grows.

Working with Suffering

Our path to growth, connection, and freedom begins with the acknowledgment of our own suffering. All spiritual traditions believe that life involves suffering. Suffering is not pain as such, but a particular kind of pain. Suffering is a painful feeling about pain. The pain of suffering is an attitude that is added to our direct experience, and that makes us feel threatened, sad, frustrated, or angry.

Suffering arises from identification with and attachment to our roles, possessions, social images, and self-definitions. When we suffer, our inherent freedom to generate possibilities and to embrace the unknown is limited by an image of a separate self composed of our past experience and our current self-image. The hope that our separate self sense will survive and the fear of its inevitable extinction keeps us turning compulsively in a circle of fascination and struggle. In this vicious circle we grab at any possibility of solidity, fight with any threat to our identity, and ignore anything that is emotionally inconvenient.

As long as we think, feel, and act as though we are a separate identity, a "me" that things happen to, we experience life as limiting and threatening. Everything appears as a potential source of pain—even those things that bring us pleasure also bring the fear of their loss. We separate ourselves from others and from life with walls of insecurity, fear, and indignation.

Suffering takes many forms. We may project it when we fear an impending event; we may linger over it when we've had a personal loss; or it may operate unacknowledged in our unconscious, manifesting as denial or numbness in the face of direct experience. It can be so habitual that pain itself becomes the theme song of our life story, the filter through which we perceive experience.

Posture of the Heart

When we think we are our body, our mind, and our feelings, we set the stage for feeling threatened, needy, and wounded by pain. These identifications are erroneous ideas about who we are. They are vanities, and they seem to require protection, care, and satisfaction.

Our identifications and our habitual reactions around them shape our stance toward life and our sense of reality. What we feel to be real about ourselves and life is the "posture of our heart." It includes who we unconsciously think we are and what we feel compelled to accept as true about life. Our heart postures move us toward whatever we consider real, and we will not stop seeking evidence to support such beliefs until our experience conforms to that reality. If we feel that disappointment and regret are real, then we will continue to push situations until we experience disappointment and regret. If we consider danger to be real, we will find evidence of threats in our environment and in our relationships. If we consider gratitude to be real, we will plumb our experience until we feel gratitude.

Our heart postures generate the stands we take about who we are and what we need to do. Our heart postures are also the standard by which we judge ourselves and validate the relevance of what we learn.

Searching for Happiness and Belonging

In our desire for happiness and a secure sense of belonging and connection, we search for satisfaction in one activity after another, one experience after another, one relationship after another, one job after another, one book after another, one look after another, and one place after another. We dance, study, fall in love, marry, have babies, buy houses, cars, stereo systems, computers, take vacations, and walk in nature. Some of us seek a path in yoga, T'ai Chi, and meditation in our attempts to find something that will make us happy and free of suffering.

There is nothing wrong or bad with any of these things, in fact, they make up much of the activity of our life. The problem is that we approach our careers, marriages, and possessions as if they contain some inherent ability to make us happy. But even if they are temporarily gratifying, none of them lasts. Like everything else in this world, they change and disappear. We feel distressed with this impermanence. Our own feelings change with new desires and we become discontented with what we have. Eventually we doubt even what we are striving for.

Our dissatisfaction is also propelled by the momentum of our seeking. In this questing mode, not only are things not inherently gratifying, but we have formed a habit of seeking. As seekers we feel tension between what we want and what we have. We fragment ourselves by suppressing impulses and feelings that do not serve our quest.

When we fragment ourselves in this way, we make the completion of our quest a prerequisite for experiencing clarity, happiness, peace, and joy, holding hostage fundamental aspects of our aliveness. By making aliveness a reward of our quest, we further rationalize and motivate that quest. We suppress and disassociate happiness in the moment, "knowing" that we will only be truly happy when we attain our goal. We need to lie about the fact that it is ourselves who linked our happiness to our goal. We keep it hostage there, waiting for our heroic rescue of it at some time in the future.

Often the short-lived gratification we do feel with an achievement is the temporary relaxation of the tension that seemed necessary in our pursuit. Even this experience of being at ease is unfamiliar. The habit of seeking reasserts itself, partly from the momentum of our past pursuing and partly from our sense that the agitation to attain something is familiar.

Our Catch 22

We also feel trapped by the impossibility of our situation. Our desire to prove our worth is continually frustrated by the methods we use for validation. We set up double-binds for ourselves. For instance, if we try to manipulate the people we love into unconditionally loving us by appearing attractive and interesting, we become testy if they respond. We try to find out if our manipulation has worked. If the manipulation worked, then we fear that they only love us because of the manipulation. If it fails, then they clearly don't love us unconditionally. We want to know now that their love is forever, while believing that it cannot possibly last. We trap ourselves in what Joseph Heller described as a "Catch 22."

> There was only one catch and that was Catch-22, which specified that a concern for one's own safety in the face of dangers that were real and immediate was the process of a rational mind. . . . Orr would be crazy to

fly more missions and sane if he didn't, but if he was sane he had to fly them. If he flew them he was crazy and didn't have to; but if he didn't want to he was sane and had to. (*Catch 22*)

The Realms of Fixation

In fact, by exploring our habits of thinking, feeling, acting, and questing, we realize that they have formed a "gestalt," a more or less coherent way of viewing reality and of behaving based on that view. Each configuration of habits is like living in a different fantasy world. For example, in one everything reminds us of loss—things smell of loss, taste flat, and lack feeling. In another world, everything recalls the emotion of anger and we feel the heat of our pain, see red everywhere, hear every word as loud alarms, and taste blood in everything. Each of these habitual worlds of pain and fixation is called a "realm."

In a realm we see the world, not as it is, but as we are. Each realm is based on the tensions, the actions and the reactions that are called "karma." These shape the way we feel and think we are, and we tend to perceive the world as a projection of our own thinking. Each realm, as a basic way of perceiving reality, is a description of a specific "karmic vision."

The realms give rise to emotional attitudes that condition our suffering. They are styles of living through which we relate to ourselves, others, and our surroundings.

In most Buddhist temples in the Himalayan kingdoms, a startling pictorial representation of the six realms of the "samsaric" (the experience of constant change and cause and effect) is prominently displayed. While it is often viewed as depicting the cycle of rebirths, and thus takes the form of a wheel, the segments also portray the six main types of unenlightened preoccupation in our worldly existence.

Each realm preoccupation is an emotional contraction—a curling up or withdrawal when dealing with change instead of an opening to aliveness and the experience of "now." The names for the realms are loose translations from sanskrit, and the realm characteristics indicate the distorting tendencies of that particular type of emotional contraction.

The six realms are:
1. the *animal* realm concerned with territory, danger and the desire to settle into a comfortable lazy stupor;
2. the *hell* realm concerned with righteousness, anger originating from a sense of victimization, and impatience with the unpredictable nature of the world;
3. the *preta* or *hungry ghost* realm concerned with what is lacking or insufficient, and with comparisons to an idealized past and idealized others;
4. the *titan* realm concerned with envy for what others have, with a sense of frustrated entitlement, and with constant struggle;
5. the *god* realm concerned with self-infatuation, pride, intoxication of fabricated experience, and indifference to others; and
6. the *human* realm concerned with the effort to possess experience, to find certainty in meaning, and to control the future through understanding and planning.

In the course of a day, we may experience the emotions and concerns of all the realms from the sense of danger characteristic of the animal realm to the pride of the god realm. Yet we also live more within one realm or a particular set of realms, and this provides each of us with a particular style of confusion and fixation that is our familiar home base.

We may notice that one or another these fixations has always been significant in our sense of ourselves and in our

The Wheel of Life

feelings about what we need to do in order to be complete and alright. We may discover that we have formed at least one identity from these concerns and have pursued a quest in order to obtain as adults whatever we felt was needed when we were younger. That felt need could be for approval, love, safety, a sense of being real, or attention. We may find that we have been playing out these quests in our work, our relationships, our friendships, and our spiritual pursuits. These preoccupations obscure reality and sacrifice our direct experience of life.

Questioning Our Assumptions

When we realize that we have made our life captive to our quest, we question our ways of seeing things and wonder whether all the assumptions we have made about ourselves and the world are really true. We entertain the possibility that our views and ways of relating are created by our own minds and not by the world. We may feel we have wasted our lives by having devoted them to worthless pursuits.

At this time there is a danger that we will feel hopeless about life, or even consider suicide. In reality, however, we now have the opportunity to consider a new life. What must end is the old way of living, not life itself.

The act of questioning how we have invested our lives indicates concern for value and the actual presence of someone who can value. Our questions interrupt our unconscious reactions and help us reflect on our habitual patterns.

Through disciplined self-observation, we can realize that we are not our patterns, our quests, our concerns, or our achievements. We use our capacity of awareness to look at the fixations that the mind has created and the body manifests. We train the reflective capacity to cut through our own mental fabrications like a precise laser beam. We realize that, perhaps, our life does not need to be a senseless struggle.

Using Suffering for Growth

With conscious work we can use our preoccupations, vanities, fixations, wounds, and quests as material from which we can mature. Our routine behaviors and the habitual stories that embellish and justify those behaviors become the opportunity for exercising clarity and expanding our attention to a more encompassing awareness. We must approach suffering through the uncompromising discipline of self-observation. We consciously examine how unconscious and habitual we are. We develop alert stillness so we can discover that our compelling concerns have no inherent reality or truth. We see clearly how these concerns arose in the past and arise in the present because we continually project our habitual preoccupations and feeling onto each new situation.

For example, if we had a complaining mother who never acknowledged us, we may have hoped that receiving acknowledgment would make us feel more real and more permanent. We may have then compulsively sought that approval from our friends, our spouse, and our co-workers. When we work consciously, we see that the energy behind our compulsive seeking and our frustrating failure to be convinced of our worth was and is an expression of our love for our wholeness. When we realize that we do not need any validation to be alive and whole, we can release our pretenses and drop our efforts to be other than we are.

Placing Attention - Developing Concentration and Insight

A simple, yet effective, foundation for conscious work is the intentional placement of attention. Practicing placement of attention is useful for calming the mind, developing concentration, and fostering insight into our thoughts and feelings. It establishes a platform of second attention from which we can practice self-observation.

Begin by sitting with a straight back and relaxed body. Bring to mind your purpose for meditating and commit yourself to keeping your attention on your meditation for however long you have decided to meditate. With your breathing even and relaxed, place your attention in the palm of one of your hands. Feel the sensations in your palm, such as heat or cold, movement of the air, movement of energy within the hand, and the texture of the air. Feel your hand touching the air and the air touching your hand. Sense the energy radiating from your palm. Keep your attention in your palm, constantly monitoring the flow and presence of sensations. When thoughts arise, let them go without giving them significance or making judgments about them, while maintaining as a constant, the second attention in your palm.

As you maintain your attention on your palm, also notice your breathing, inner and outer sounds, and images that come to mind. Notice that you can attend to two things at once. Your constant attention rests in the sensations in your palm while other things come and go.

Imagine yourself as a calm lake in which the thoughts and feelings that arise are bubbles that burst at the surface as they meet the clear sky. They come and go from moment to moment as you maintain yourself as the lake of attention. Treat expectations, plans, frustrations, and hopes as bubbles that pass away when they meet the surface of your consciousness.

Do this meditation for ten minutes, increasing the period of sitting as the capacity and ease with sitting meditation develops. This type of meditation can also be done by focusing on the breath, placing the attention on the sensations of the nostrils feeling the texture of the breath as it enters and leaves the body.

In summary, developing real insight means becoming familiar with our own states of mind, and learning how our thoughts, attitudes and feelings produce our pain and suffering. The ideas and practices presented in this book draw on a long tradition of work and can help us cultivate the awareness and energies that bring radiance and happiness to our lives.

In the chapters that follow, consciously step into the mythology and into each realm as your familiar home, feeling the sensations of living within that frame of mind, and recognizing these patterns in your own life. Note what is there, the reactive efforts that are made, and the creative possibilities that could be realized with conscious work. If you discover that you are rooted in one particular style, notice how the others relate to that one and are enlisted in the service of your identification with its attributes. Unconscious identification is a source of suffering. Deliberate conscious identification develops our witness capacity and frees us from the compelling grip of the past and of habits.

3

Avalokiteshvara

The Myth of
the Great Compassionate One

The seat of the soul is there, where the outer and the
inner worlds meet.

Novalis

What we're seeking is an experience of being alive,
so that our life experiences on the purely physical
plane will have resonances within our own inner-
most being and reality, so that we actually feel the
rapture of being alive.

Joseph Campbell

THE MYTH OF AVALOKITESHVARA, the great Bodhisattva (someone who dedicates himself to relieving the suffering of all sentient beings), presents the ideal of compassion
and the path of compassion in a multi-dimensional way. Myths
are distilled metaphors that provide a structure for understanding our experience. While we relate to the story of a myth
on a conscious level, the language of metaphor used in myth
speaks directly to the unconscious at several levels.

Mythology and the Inner World of the Body

The stories and teachings of the tantric traditions on which this book is based cannot be taken as mere intellectual explorations, or they will lose their spiritual power and lead to confusion. Joseph Campbell, one of the great contemporary thinkers about mythology, explains the "wonder-land" of myth in the following way: "From the outer world the senses carry images to the mind, which do not become myth until there transformed by fusion with accordant insights, awakened as imagination from the inner world of the body."

The myth of Avalokiteshvara, like many myths, contains actual formulas for inner work. However, these formulas can be realized only when we have been prepared by appropriate spiritual practice and are able to open both our mind and energy body to receive and assimilate the teachings hidden within the story of the myth. Then the metaphors or symbols of the myth organize and direct our experience. They open channels of awareness and energy that are latent in us but are not easily unlocked without conscious work.

In this way the truth of a myth depends on its usefulness as a guide to inner space. The value of this guidance is determined by our preparation and the use that we, as practitioners, make of its materials. To the extent that we can experience and embody the work in the myth, we develop new habits of seeing, hearing and feeling. We think, feel, and act in new ways.

The practice of working consciously with myth not only helps us to organize our understanding of the world, but also to embody the abstract in our concrete experience. For instance, when we hear that the hero or heroine descends into a cave of despair before emerging into the light with renewed resources, we can feel our own heartache as we submerge ourselves in our emotions. When we do this consciously and with the understanding that the heart breaks before growth occurs, we realize the vitality of our intense feelings. We experience all the stages of our emotions—from shock through intensity to release and realignment—and we feel the freshness of new experiences as we open to the growth that follows. Myths portray the journeys of the hero or heroine from innocence, through perils and challenges, to the rewards of union, splendor and peace. As we know from grieving for a lost parent, friend, or loved one, we grow through the stages of grief and recovery, arriving once more at aliveness.

Initially, the myth helps us to understand something about the nature of our everyday experience, as well as birth, death, change, and our relationship to the world. Later we realize that, at another level, it gives us a window onto experiences beyond our everyday existence. It guides us toward the embodiment of harmony, splendor, wisdom, love and compassion, beyond merely representing those extraordinary capacities in the mind. As Campbell says: "The metaphor of myth and poetry suggests the actuality that hides behind the visible aspect. The metaphor is the mask of God through which eternity is to be experienced."

Avalokita - The Great Compassionate One

Mythologically, the Great Compassionate One, Avalokiteshvara (Avalokita)—also known as Chenrezig in Tibet, Kuan Yin in China, and Kannon in Japan —was a being who lived before human history, attained a very high state of enlightenment, and chose to work for the benefit of others rather than pass into the ultimate blissful state. While Avalokita was neither male nor female, this Bodhisattva was referred to as a male in the original Buddhist mythology of India, and we will continue that custom for the purposes of this story, keeping in mind that wisdom qualities are beyond gender.

The Sutras (ancient Buddhist texts containing the dialogues and discourses of the Buddha) contain many stories about Avalokiteshvara's ability to manifest wisdom and compassion. What follows in this chapter and in the introductions to the each of the realms of suffering in Part II are not translations but freely told exerpts from stories about him.

As we enter these stories, we can imagine ourselves as characters in the story. We particularly want to feel ourselves embody the qualities of the Great Compassionate One. If we observe and experience the world as Avalokiteshvara, we can experience transcending wisdom and feel the energy of compassion.

Birth

Avalokita, according to some versions, was born from a ray of light from the right eye of Boundless Radiance, Amitabha, who is the light that creates the entire universe. At birth, he immediately uttered the sacred words *OM MANI PADME HUM (Hail the Great Wisdom Jewel in the Heart of the Lotus).* Later, having reached the point of enlightenment, he looked with the penetrating eye of wisdom at the suffering in the universe and said, "I have attained many powers, and rather than leave this all behind by dissolving into the Essence, I want to save all these beings from their condition of suffering, because I cannot see them as different from myself."

The Promise

He looked at the various worlds of suffering, and made a vow to Amitabha. "I am going to ease the suffering of all the realms until the job is finished and, if I do not succeed, may my head split open like a coconut." He put everything on the line to accomplish his goal.

He began his work in the hell realm to relieve the suffering of the hell fiends. He used all the miraculous lights and magical

Avalokiteshvara

sounds that he could generate. In three days, six hours, and twenty-three minutes he cleaned out the hells.

As he was about to move on to the next realm of the pretas, the humans alone had filled up the hells again in two days, five hours and fifty-six minutes. He saw this phenomenon occurring at a rate that was faster than his own ceaseless work and was beside himself. "This is too much! I don't know if I can do this." Avalokiteshvara became discouraged and quit.

At this point his father, Boundless Radiance, who remembered his vow, tapped Avalokiteshvara on the top of his head. His head cracked and split and he felt enormous pain. Then Boundless Radiance said to Avalokiteshvara, "If you like, I will relieve you of the headache so you can pass into Nirvana."

Avalokiteshvara replied, "No. The headache woke me up. When I look back at the realms, my heartache is much greater than my headache. So I will keep the headache and I'll keep working to free all beings."

Boundless Radiance was so impressed with Avalokiteshvara's determination that he hit him on the head a few more times. Each time Amitabha struck, a new head appeared, many of which had three faces. Each face radiated the clarity of compassion that could liberate beings. For those beings who were particularly stubborn, one of the heads near the top was that of the wrathful Lord of Death. Then Amitabha put his own head at the very top of the Compassionate One.

To further increase his capacity, Avalokiteshvara began to sprout arms. First he grew four, then six, and then eight, and finally a thousand arms, like the brilliant aura of infinite rays of light. In the center of each hand was an eye to see the suffering of all beings, representing the consciousness of love combined with wisdom. This equipped Avalokiteshvara for the task of bringing compassion into existence. In addition, the Great Compassionate One could take on any form, from that of an atom to that of animals and human beings, including our form. From that time forth, there was still suffering in the universe, but compassion also existed, along with the possibility of the end of suffering.

Avalokita Reveals a Path to Enlightenment

In his book, *Bodhisattva of Compassion*, Blofeld relates the story, from the Surangama Sutra, in which Avalokita, addressing an assembly presided over by the Buddha and made up of human and divine beings, reveals how he attained enlightenment through meditation on sound. "Mentally detaching hearing from its object and then eliminating both those concepts, he had at first perceived that both disturbance and stillness are illusory and next came to realize the non-existence even of that rarified perception." Blofeld continues, quoting the Sutra, "'As non-existent, both subject (hearer or hearing) and object (sound) are merged in the Void, and awareness of voidness becomes all-embracing. When awareness of both existence and non-existence vanishes, Nirvana supervenes.'" With this kind of realization, Avalokiteshvara acquired both the compassion that arises from the profound wisdom of the nature of ultimate reality and the ability to feel the struggles of all beings floundering in their ocean of delusion.

Another lesson that the story reveals to us concerns the nature of "mantra" as a combination of words and sound. The sanskrit word "mantra" comes from "man," meaning "to think," and "tra," meaning "tool." Thus mantra refers to "tools for thinking" or "instruments that develop thinking." Avalokiteshvara did not simply express the famous mantra *OM MANI PADME HUM,* but developed the practice into a form of listening. As mentioned above, the key to his enlightenment was revealed through his listening. This listening not only activates specific energy patterns in us (one of the purposes and effects of mantra practice), but also dissolves all boundaries and self-imposed assumptions.

When we listen and reflect on the nature of sound, we cannot locate sound. When a bell is rung, is the sound in the bell? In our ear? In our head? In the space between us and the bell? We cannot find the sound. This inquiry can give us insights into the nature of reality and the emptiness on which Avalokiteshvara expounded.

The words of the mantra *OM MANI PADME HUM* also reveal profound meaning. *OM* does not have a simple or translatable meaning. It is generally taken to refer to the universal, representing the individual expanding to the level of the universal. *MANI* means jewel, or wish-granting jewel. It is closely related to the word "manas," which means "mind" in the sense of intelligence and the intellectual and mental faculties of consciousness. *PADME* means lotus or heart of the lotus (as well as the lotus in the Heart Center). The lotus represents the true nature of beings, unstained by the mud of the world of pain and illusions, whose blossom reaches for the heavens through the murkiest of ponds, remaining dry even when surrounded by water. The realization of this true nature is attained through the path of the Great Compassionate One, Avalokiteshvara. *HUM* is a syllable without precise translation that represents the principle of the universal manifesting in the individual. It conveys the sense of surrender by the individual to the flow of the universal. We recognize not only that the Essence or ultimate nature of life operates through and within us, but that this is true for all beings and situations. As Lama Govinda points out in his book *Foundations of Tibetan Mysticism* (a detailed presentation of the meaning and practice of this mantra), "*OM MANI PADME HUM* is the highest expression of that wisdom of the heart, that courageously descends into

the world—and even into the deepest hells—in order to transform the poison of death (separation) into the Elixir of Life."

This profound wisdom does not engender a feeling of
superiority toward those who are unrealized, but reveals the
essential equality of all beings. In this way we can recognize
ourselves in others and place ourselves in the place of others,
knowing their basic goodness, their pains, and their true
aspirations.

Avalokiteshvara represents our compassionate desire to
relieve the suffering that we experience as our everyday world.
By predicating our feelings, thoughts, and actions on the idea
of individual separateness and self-identity, we experience life
as limited, painful, and imperfect in its incessantly changing
conditions. The resulting insecurity and fear place walls of
ignorance around us, separating us from others and from the
realization of aliveness. Avalokiteshvara, realizing our essential oneness, is the dedicated energy that seeks to awaken us to
all the states of mind in which we live. These states of mind,
these domains or realms of experience, are the illusory constructs that must be dissolved if we wish to be alive and free.

The Forms that Avalokiteshvara Takes in the Realms of Suffering

Being able to take any form, Avalokiteshvara appears in
each realm as manifestation of wisdom appropriate to the form
of preoccupation that characterizes the realm. He goes from
one realm to the next, taking on the aspects and image that will
awaken the beings in each realm to their aliveness and their
true nature. Each of the chapters on the realms of suffering in
Part II is introduced by a vignette describing the beings in that
realm, who represent aspects of our suffering, and the wisdom
manifestations of Avalokiteshvara in the forms of the Spiritual
Father and the Divine Mother.

Avalokiteshvara helps us, as suffering beings caught in the realm, not by acting as an external force, but by awakening a force within us. This force, which is activated by heart energy and the example of the Great Compassionate One, enables us to meet each situation fearlessly and use it as a means of liberation. We feel connected both to suffering beings and realized teachers through our heartache and desire for freedom. The powers of light and spiritual oneness arise in our heart center as Avalokiteshvara acts through us and takes our form.

The story of Avalokiteshvara reminds us of those parts of us that hate suffering and have genuine compassion for others. The Great Compassionate One guides us in using our capacity for compassion to discover our own essential nature, allowing us to achieve aliveness, connection, wholeness and freedom.

Meditation

The meditations that follow comprise a four-step process to help us develop our own wisdom qualities. First, we evoke the qualities we want to awaken by stating our desire for clarity and freedom. Second, we relate this desire to our own habitual suffering. Third, we turn our attention to others by expanding our awareness to encompass their suffering, becoming a beneficial presence in their lives by radiating joy to them. Finally, we release our efforts and relax into our natural self.

Aspiration Prayer

The first meditation is an aspiration prayer that can be recited aloud or read silently as an opening to other meditations, and serves to invite the wisdom energy of the Great Compassionate One into our lives.

Aspiration Prayer For Oneself and Others
To the Great Compassionate One

With the Heart-Posture of utmost gratitude to the Compassion-Embodying Presence that transverses limitless space, that is informed by the Wisdom of Essence, that participates in the world through contributions that are dedicated to the Truest Aim, that arises in relationship to me as teachers, teachings, support, and spiritual community, and with dedicated attention to my connection with all beings and to the rare auspicious opportunity to receive profound teachings, may I swiftly actualize the Compassion of Avalokiteshvara and Radiate the True Freedom that benefits all.

May all projections appear transparent with Avalokiteshvara as the light that shines through them.

When, under the influence of fear, desire, and numbness, I see confused states as something good and grow attached to the projections thus created, Avalokiteshvara open the eyes of my heart's Wisdom and unite me with the Jewel Essence of my human birthright.

When I, as a moth is attracted to a hot light, see Samsara as happiness and ceaselessly invoke the causes of sorrow with my body, speech, and mind; Avalokiteshvara give me Reflective Pause that I may interrupt these meaningless actions.

When I hide, fight, and fall into lazy stupor, like some animals, protecting an illusion of what is mine in ignorance; Avalokiteshvara light the torch of Spacious Wisdom that I may see boundaries as relationship and boundlessness as Wisdom Essence.

When I burn in the hells of suffering as a victim, consumed by hatred, anger, blame, and guilt; Avalokiteshvara bring the water of love and fresh Rain of Compassion and dispel the fires and guide me in the natural flow of life's precious river.

When I am consumed by unsatiable wants, dissatisfying comparisons, and the pure frustrating pain of wanting; Avalokiteshvara loosen the knots of my clinging that my own hands may generate an endless stream of treasures.

When I suffer jealously and fight helplessly to attain that which I feel others have and is owed me; Avalokiteshvara blow the cool, Fresh Wind of Harmony to block the currents of envy.

When I heedlessly bask in the delights of gods, unmindful of the passing years, uncaring about the suffering of others, denying the nature of life and of Essence; Avalokiteshvara provide a carrier of Compassion, Wonder, and Insight that I may cross the ocean of desire.

When I am hooked on understanding, addicted to self-criticism, fixated on ownership of the future, and seeking a secure harbor of meaning away from the waves of birth, sickness, change, old age, confusion, and death; Avalokiteshvara grant me the Wisdom of Equanimity and the Jewel of Direct Experience.

By the Power of the Compassionate Presence of
    Avalokiteshvara,
By the Power of True Intention,
By the Power of the Forces hereby Invoked,
By the Power of the Unknown,
By the Power of Heartfelt Dedication,
By the Virtue of Practice and Dedicated Living,
By the Truth of all these, may this Aspiration for the
    Happiness and Freedom of All be quickly accomplished.
OM MANI PADME HUM HRI

(This short Aspiration Prayer to the Great Compassionate One was written for myself and others by Martin Lowenthal, a grateful student of Lar Short and follower of the Way of Radiance. May this only bring peace and benefit to all beings.)

Compassionate Presence Meditation

Before we can be a loving presence to others, we must experience being loved by and compassionate toward ourselves. The second meditation develops our sense of a loving and compassionate presence in our life.

1. Sit in a comfortable and alert posture.

2. Imagine that standing behind you is someone who loves you very much.

3. Sense his or her loving gaze upon you.

4. Perhaps he/she is about to speak to you or touch you in a loving way.

5. Allow yourself to be physically organized—adjusting your posture, energy and feelings—in their loving presence and feel the sensations that arise as you allow yourself to relax into this love.

6. Allow your mind to relax imagining that you are in a vast, open, and beautiful space.

7. Consider that this loving presence is simply an agent of love itself.

8. Continue to relax your mind even further, feeling surrounded by love itself.

9. Allow yourself to be physically organized in the presence of love itself and feel the sensations that arise in your body.

10. Consider that love itself is an aspect of the Divine.

11. Allow yourself to be physically organized in the presence of the Divine and feel the sensations that arise.

12. Allow your mind to relax even further, considering that—whether you remember it or not—you are always physically in the presence of the Divine.
13. As you arise from this meditation, consider that all forms that you perceive are the body of the Divine, that all vibrations, sounds, and sensations that you feel are the voice of the Divine, and that all thoughts, emotions, and mental activities arise as clouds that come and go in the sky-like awareness of the heart of the Divine.
14. Continue to cultivate this awareness in all your activities. Especially invoke this awareness at the beginning of any meditation practice, giving attention to the sensations that arise.

Progressive Relaxation into Self

Like a muscle, our spirit needs stretching, effort, and relaxation. We stretch into the unknown; we make the effort to use life experience as nourishment; and we relax into our natural condition. Before we can realize our essential oneness, we need to dissolve the boundaries of our various self-definitions and defenses. Some approaches to this process involve breaking through such walls by intense effort. Others use our capacity for release as a way of relaxing into our essential nature. The following meditation is one way of doing the latter.

1. Place attention on the outermost sense of self in the body.
2. Inhale. On the exhalation, releasing tensions in this outer layer of self, relax into a smaller, interior sense of self.
3. Inhale and relax again on the exhalation into a still smaller, more interior sense of self. Repeat this process until the sense of self coalesces into a small drop at the heart.

4. Continue to repeat the process as the drop gets smaller and more concentrated until it disappears and the sense of self becomes pure awareness. Abide.
5. As a self-sense arises, feel the boundaries of that self at that moment and begin the process again until the self dissolves into pure awareness.
6. After repeating this process several times, close the meditation with a dedication, radiating out the benefits of the meditation to all beings with the heartfelt wish that they may all swiftly realize true freedom from suffering.

PART II

*From the Realms of Suffering
to the Wisdom of Aliveness*

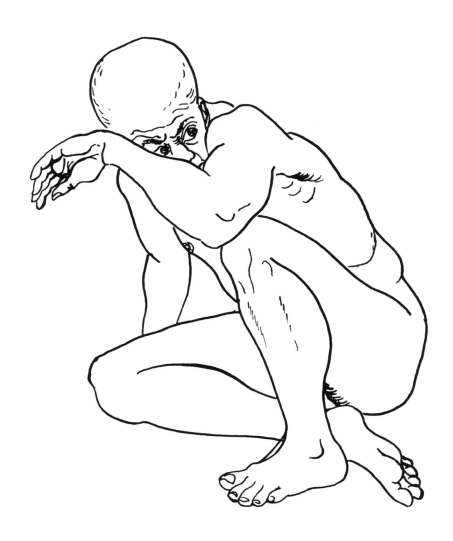

4

Beyond the Territorial Imperative

From the Animal Realm to the Dynamic of Relating

Hell is other people.

Jean Paul Sartre, Huis Clos

To a worm in horseradish, the whole world is horse-radish.

Yiddish Proverb

I destroy my enemy by making him my friend.

Abraham Lincoln

We must learn to live together as brothers or perish together as fools.

John F. Kennedy

The animal realm is inhabited by beings who bark and bite at any intruder, protecting their turf and fighting to be left alone. They lay around in a lazy stupor, wanting to be petted and touched but afraid and skittish. Many of them are phobic about unknown things and chaotic situations. They want to settle into a cozy space of their own with predictable routines. Others are obsessed with dangers, afraid of the demands of relationships and the unpredictability of having others in their lives. They long for love and attention, but are terrified of intimacy and responsibility.

Avalokiteshvara enters this realm in a variety of forms. As the Buddha with a book he educates, and as Prajnaparamita, the grace-filled wisdom, she invites the frightened beings to learn and grow. As wrathful deities (joy beings who appear in a wrathful mood), he wakes up the numbed beings to a sense of immediacy. He delivers a shock that inflicts a pause, interrupting their stories and penetrating the protectiveness of their identities. The mother Dakinis, another way in which Avalokita manifests, startle and move the animal beings with their own elemental forces. They invite the lazy beings out of their territories into activity and relationship.

W HEN WE OCCUPY the animal realm, our awareness is dominated by our desire to possess territory. Animals attempt to bind and possess space with urine, growls and bared teeth. As animals, we use a favorite word—"mine."

Possession and Territory

When we possess a space, we identify ourselves with that space. We would like our territory to be as solid as the earth and hope it will give us a sense of permanence in an ever-changing world. At some level we feel that if we could keep the good things in life and dispense with the bad, we could then get beyond the conditions of our life. We could be more open and free. The underlying assumption is that we can create permanence by attaching ourselves to familiar possessions and routines; and that once we feel secure from the threatening changes in the world, we can begin to live.

In our attempt to secure the familiar, we mark our territory to distinguish it from the territory of others. Since we define the world in terms of good and bad, attempting to possess good things and avoid bad, we become suspicious of others who might want our goods or could contaminate our space with something bad. We erect barriers of privacy around our room, our office, our time, and our meditation space. These boundaries, established for our protection, become our prison walls, separating us from the riches of relationships, discovery, and the world around us.

Heart Postures of Vulnerability and Fear

In our efforts to protect ourselves from threats to our turf, we become paranoid. Our heart posture is that we and our stuff are vulnerable and that fear is the appropriate way of relating to a dangerous world. The world is filled with people who disturb, threaten and pollute us and our possessions. We constantly employ a kind of radar to alert us to potential intrusions into our space and interruptions of our routines. We put out signals to let other people know what is ours and how and when we do things. When we are in this frame of mind, all we want is security and comfort. We want the comfort of love, hoping it will make us feel connected, but we want it on our own terms so we do not feel threatened by the relationship.

Our natural energy and awareness stiffen into a territory of the mind, characterized by ignorance of the world and an inability to discriminate. This mentality looks directly ahead as if wearing blinders, and attempts to adjust each situation for comfort. It tries to make events conform to our expectations in order to feel secure. In this realm, we see everything as a potential threat or intrusion. Although we yearn for contact to overcome our loneliness, relationships that do exist are ignored, new ones are rarely sought, and when interaction does take place, an overriding concern with maintaining boundaries governs our attention and our activity.

Laziness

Another characteristic of the animal realm is laziness—a lack of energy to properly care for ourselves. We are unwilling to look at situations or ourselves from different points of view, fearing that this might compromise our inner boundaries, our self-image.

In the animal realm we are afraid to examine our styles of relating to ourselves and the world. Our concern is to maintain self-boundaries and self-respect. We can be very stubborn and serious in maintaining our turf and pursuing our goals, and we lack the sense of perspective that comes from self-reflective humor. In this realm humor is awkward and used to relieve tension. It is a tool of release or manipulation rather than an open, reflective way of relating to the predictability of our habits and the unpredictability of the world. True humor is threatening because it cuts through our self-deceptive attempts at maintaining rigid identity.

Avoiding Intrusion, Ignoring Relationships, and Seeking Security

In this drive for security, comfort and contact on our own terms, we try to avoid intrusion and threats to our world. We are afraid of change and of the effort it takes to learn new behaviors and develop new rules. We shy away from the struggle in order to survive, to be safe, and to establish comfortable new expectations.

In this contraction of attention we ignore our basic relationship to others, to society and to the world. We do not perceive the interdependent nature of our existence. We forget our reliance on the efforts of others for food, shelter, clothing and our environment. We ignore the fact that we do not inherently exist as an independent entity. We are blind to the relative nature of existence, to the moment-to-moment reality of death, and to the fact that we are always in relationship to others, whether we acknowledge it or not.

Wanting Connection and Fearing Contact

In this realm we long to be taken care of, yet fear relationships. We hunger for touch, but fear contact. We think we would be okay if people left us alone, but, when they do, we feel abandoned. Trying to resolve this double-bind of fear and longing, we invite other people to be with us, but only on our terms and if they respect our boundaries.

Addiction to Familiarity

We establish familiar boundaries and routines in order to ward off the wounds of physical discomfort, pain and abandonment. We blot out both our past and any real sense of a future. Present fears and well-being are the center of our attention. We fear the risks of real relationship and comfort ourselves with our own space, our own schedule and our own sacred objects. We cling to the known whenever possible, and shun the unknown and unfamiliar.

We soothe ourselves with pets—animals that are domesticated and loyal. Pets spend their lives sleeping, playing and being fed, and are, above all, ours. Familiar things such as our favorite armchair, an elegant wine glass, and grandmother's china become sacred objects, and we make their use into a ritual.

Spiritual Masquerade of the Hermit

Animal realm aspects affect our spiritual work. We practice in isolation, preferring our cave to sitting with the community. The underlying principles of the teachings seem confusing, and we meditate in familiar, ritualistic ways, surrounded by objects and pictures that make us feel at home. We make our teacher into a savior or parent figure who protects us and does all the exploration for us. We follow like sheep, without doubting or deciding anything for ourselves, under the guise of devotion. We become rigid in our practice routines and in our devotion, protecting our spiritual work from the world and the possibility of confusion.

Underlying Dynamic of Relating

Each realm is the contracted, cringing, clinging reaction to a radiant spiritual process of aliveness called a dynamic. Underlying the animal preoccupation with position and boundaries is the essential dynamic of relating. When boundaries are recognized as lines of connection, not of exclusion, we see our connections to the world around us and our relationship to those who are a part of our world.

We see that boundaries and identities are relative and realize that they are always changing. We begin to discriminate between the various kinds of boundaries and identities in the world and to understand that they have cycles of growth and decay. Thich Nhat Hanh, a Vietnamese Zen Master and poet, illustrates this by suggesting that we consider a rose and garbage. The rose appears beautiful and pure and the garbage ugly and smelly. Yet, in a matter of weeks, the rose will wilt and decay and become garbage, and the garbage may become flowers and vegetables. "Looking at a rose you can see the garbage and looking at the garbage you can see a rose." He calls this "interbeing."

As we work with our habits of exclusion and fear, we sense this interbeing and see ourselves in others and others in ourselves. We commune with others through the understanding that we are all subject to the same principles of life, and that life is a changing and relative existence in which we are all dependent upon one another. Every person becomes a mirror, every interaction a realization of the human design, and every boundary a connection and reminder of spaciousness.

Hosting not Hiding

We start to realize that we can take responsibility for ourselves and our connections with others. We can enjoy our territory as a place for hosting rather than hiding. We can act in terms of the community of which we are a part.

Every being radiates its own freshness and aliveness. Although we are often closed to this radiance, we recognize it when we see a baby—dynamic, direct, vulnerable, responsive and alive. In that moment, we feel our own aliveness more completely and we accept the baby exactly as it is. A genuine smile generates the same feeling.

Learning

We can come to understand in these experiences that, while all things change and security is elusive, basic radiance cannot be destroyed. It simply takes different forms in relationship to other radiant forms. Relating, as a life process, opens up our space and allows us to include and dance with another. As our space becomes more flexible and expansive, we give up some of the familiar in order to explore and embrace more of the unknown. In a sense, we die to our old space—our old boundaries and definitions—in order to open to a bigger space. This openness is the key ingredient in learning. When we see life as an opportunity to learn, we form a foundation for growth; it is the fundamental characteristic of aliveness, and of our design as human beings.

This foundation creates the space, the context, for the other dynamics and wisdom qualities to develop. Each of them in turn enhances the process of growth and realization of spaciousness. Opening to the unknown is essential for the development of any form of wisdom, and every new realization cracks us open a bit more, expanding our capacity to grow.

Wisdom of Spaciousness

We develop the jewel of spacious wisdom when we experience the boundless space out of which all things arise. Opening, learning and growing are the foundations for developing the spacious awareness that frees us. We sense our own essence and begin to awaken to our Essence Self. We realize that our personality is our unique expression of our Self nature, the Self in Essence that is beyond our personal self. An acorn has all the elements necessary to become an oak tree, even though we cannot know how many branches or leaves it will have. So, too, we each embody the design of spiritual realization, even though the individual form it takes may differ. The *nature* of that realization, however, will be the same for each individual expression: there is nothing to prove, disprove, approve or improve.

When we operate out of our Essence Self, we are simply ourselves. It is not that we know who or what that Self is—it is always changing—but we are not trying to be anyone other than who we are in any given moment. We realize that the purpose of life is for living—nothing else—and we live our lives now.

Stepping Beyond Ourselves

We develop the awakened qualities of this dynamic of relating by practicing meditation, community service, and dedication. We want to observe, discriminate, choose and relate to other people. The first step in this process is a simple pause, an interruption in the habitual course of thinking, feeling and acting that gives us an opportunity to reflect.

The pause is a critical ingredient in developing our spiritual capacity. The animal aspect in us operates by a stimulus/response mechanism. However, as a human being we have the additional capacity to create a pause. When we react with stimulus/response, we can then add a pause for reflection, creating the sequence of stimulus/response/pause/reflection. After a while we begin to have the quality of anticipation that can be expressed as stimulus/pause/response/pause/reflection. With anticipation, we no longer simply react; we open to the stimulus before responding and in this way we can develop choice.

In spiritual work we learn to experience, extend and explore that pause as part of the process of awakening. Eventually we realize that the pause, when not hidden by incessant activity of the mind and body, is always there. It is characterized by heightened awareness—the continuous background of all experience and action. Then stimulus and response are seen to arise within the pause.

Greater freedom follows from this growing awareness. We have more choice about the pause, about another course of action, and about the variety of ways we can relate to each situation. We are free to be and to act with aliveness rather than being pushed and pulled by automatic responses. We are free to grant significance to something other than the stimulus and response. By opening to the pause, we grant significance to it, the space within which stimuli arise and responses are played out.

Meditating with a Partner

In combination with the practices presented in the previous chapters, the following meditation with a partner is particularly useful in working with the mental and emotional frames that keep us mired in this realm.

As you and your partner sit opposite each other, sense your boundaries—where you feel that your space stops and your partners begins. Do this first with your eyes closed and then

Meditating with a Partner

with them open. Notice any assumptions you are making about yourself and the other person and where you experience points of connection.

Then alter your frame of reference for the situation. Change your assumptions about your partner. For example, imagine that your partner is threatening and notice your reactions. Try other thoughts such as, "This person is angry with me," "This person is trying to help me," "This person loves me," and "This person is a friend and someone I can trust." Notice that your thoughts about the other person affect your sense of boundaries and connections to your partner. Be sure that the final assumption that is used is a pleasant one.

Conclude the exercise by placing your attention in your heart center, filling it with an inner smile, and radiating that smiling energy to your partner. Simultaneously, receive his/her smiling energy so that the two of you are mutually sending and receiving radiance from each other. Then, along with your partner, radiate that energy out into the world.

By opening the territories of our mind, we arrive at the well-being and connection that we were trying to achieve through our possessiveness. We wanted to feel connected to something and to assert that we have a place in the world. When we open to relating to other people, we discover that the constant giving and receiving in the moment leads to a more authentic belonging. Through love we gain the whole world, making old enemies into new friends.

5

Against the Tide
In the Hell Realm

The Power of Pain,
the Pain of Powerlessness
and the Freedom of Emptiness

Hell is oneself,
Hell is alone, the other figures in it
Merely projections. There is nothing to escape from
And nothing to escape to.
One is always alone.

T. S. Eliot, The Cocktail Party

Because when a man is in turmoil
How shall he find peace
Save by staying patient till the stream clears?
How can a man's life keep its course
If he will not let it flow?

Tao Te Ching, 15

In the Hell Realm, Avalokiteshvara encounters beings who are *suffering in a variety of ways from the results of their preoccupation with anger, frustration, hatred, victimness, guilt, and blame, and who see others as tormentors or potential tormentors. Some are imploding and freezing from cold anger and hatred. Others are exploding from hot anger and frustration. Still others are being cut by knife-like anger and are licking the blood of their own wounds, as they are hung by guilt. All are wishing they had the power to exorcise the demons of thoughts, feelings, and wounds.*

To beings in this realm, Avalokita appears as Aksobhya (the Spiritual Father) and Locana (the Divine Mother). Aksobhya, his body space blue, enters the realm on a great elephant radiating the colorless, pure, white light of mirror-like wisdom. He holds a mirror in which beings must reflect upon themselves and their self-judgments. They realize that their thoughts and emotions are passing images and that the mirror itself represents their own essential qualities of clarity and unperturbability, a nature unaffected and untouched by the phenomena being reflected. He represents the wisdom capacity for patience and clarity, undisturbed by disgust or anger. As he greets the beings in Hell with patience, he is not reactive and his presence is not conditioned. He listens to them without becoming entangled in their tales of woe and long histories of victimization. His symbol is the vajra which symbolizes the indestructible, diamond-like nature of reality—spotless and pure.

The Divine Mother Locana is the "Seeing One," the one with the Buddha Eye. She sees each person's real nature. Even though the inhabitants of hell may be suffering painfully and their anger may be tremendously violent, she sees their Essence natures and relates to them as beings who are inherently free and separate from their past experiences and present conditions. She invites them to take that view of themselves—to see themselves not simply in terms of the reflections in the mirror but of the mirror itself. She encourages them to see fire and water not as something to burn and drown in but to purify and cleanse the different fears and obscurities. She also indicates to them that fire and water are part of the alchemy of rebirth, a way to transform pain, anger and hostility.

EVERY SELF-IMAGE is a contraction of our natural dynamic qualities. We try to stop the intolerable flux of the unknown by clutching a "permanent" identity. We distort our perceptions to protect the fragile self-image we have created. In the hell realm, we identify ourselves as victims. Our thoughts are filled with pain, blame, righteousness and aggression.

Power of Pain

When we inhabit this realm, we operate from a sense of being trapped in a hostile world. We "know" that something is terribly wrong. Something needs to be fixed, saved, or liberated. Existence is problematic.

We think that at some earlier time in our lives we were wounded and, because of the pain of that wound, we are disfigured. Our life history is a tale of the wounds and pain that we have suffered again and again. "Not again" is our theme, sometimes said pleadingly, sometimes defiantly.

Our psycho-emotional blood fascinates us. We feed on our own wounds, savoring the blood and severed flesh as if it were food—it seems so real, so tasty, so full of insights. We wash down our bloody meal with tears that seem refreshing, thinking they must be the true rain of blessings.

In this realm pain is the proof of reality. If we experience pain, then an injury must be real. We contract further, creating more pain, thereby reinforcing our sense of being wounded again and again. If this pattern persists, the wound becomes the center or organizing principle of our life. Then comes the search for a solution, the "quest."

Seeking a Way Out

This quest for a solution to the problem of our existence actually becomes a further problem. A quest is not necessarily destructive, but when it defines life as a problem to be solved, it perpetuates and reinforces the problem perspective. Many so-called spiritual quests are pursued under the guise of salvation or escape from evil. But the true quest is for authenticity, not rescue; for freedom, not the prison of righteousness; for harmony, not the conflict of retribution; for openness, not the security of familiar wounds.

When we are fixed in our identity, everything flows around us and into us. We feel surrounded by change and battered by events. "If things would simply leave me alone, I would be fine." Yet if we remove ourselves from relationships and the world, we feel lost and alone. All this feels unfair.

We think: "I am not strong enough or good enough to survive; the universe is stacked against me. Everything has been created to destroy me. Even if it was not deliberately created to destroy me, that is what it does. I simply try to mind my own business, and everything is pulling, pushing, and beating on me."

Hatred

Anger arises and congeals as hatred, which can be viewed as anger projected over time. Anger can be directed inward at the self, which is too weak to maintain its identity. Or it can be directed outward at an unfair universe that lacks compassion and destroys what we are identified with. Often it is aimed in both directions. This is the root of hell, resisting the flow of the universe and feeling utterly separate from it. Then we feel too weary to stand against that flow, which is breaking us down, or we feel outraged because it seems to be destroying who we think we are. It does not occur to us that these changes and events are the very things that gave rise to us, and that sustain us from moment to moment.

Aggression and Victimness

We also develop a posture of aggression toward the pain, ourselves, and whatever we project as the cause of the pain. We want to scratch violently at the wound as if to tear it away and to strike out at the world where wounds can occur.

Relating through aggression renders the entire universe a place in which there are always victims and victimizers. Aggression becomes a frame of reference through which all social situations are seen. Blame, anger and hatred energize this point of view, and propel our reactions as self-proclaimed victims.

The Righteousness of Blame

Blame preoccupies the occupants of hell. Either the world is responsible for our problems, or we are. We feel like victims of a painfully unfair life. Our most intense emotions are anger, rage, fear, or hatred. Our moral stance is righteousness.

This hatred is a form of self-hatred. Even our hatred for other people is tied to qualities that we hate in ourselves or to those we hate ourselves for fearing. We move from one form of self-hatred to another—from guilt (feeling that we are to blame), to shame (feeling that we are not good enough), to weakness (feeling that we are victims).

In this realm we assert, "Life is unfair and nobody deserves my situation. It is wrong." The life questions in this realm are: "How can I make myself safe from the unfair pain of life?" and "How can I prove to the world that I do not deserve to be hurt?" The filters of perception are: "How are others and life failing me?" and "How do I fail myself by my own terrible shortcomings?"

No matter how good our social image, our physical self-image, and our professional self-image are, they never seem quite good enough. We could always be better, and circumstances are always changing. We judge ourselves like an irascible god who sees our failures and criticizes our successes.

Desire for the Power

In addition, we feel inadequate because we are not powerful enough—not powerful enough to stop injustice, failure, or pain. We erect our righteousness on the cornerstone of powerlessness. At least we can define the terms of what is right even if we cannot control the flow of life. All the while, our desire for power grows. We want to destroy the causes of pain, even if they turn out to be ourselves.

Beyond aggression, we wish for heaven, a god realm in which there is eternal peace and no disturbance. We try to become God in order to control the disturbance, or become at least the friend of God and get God to control the world so we can feel secure.

Consider a young girl whose father dies. If she is four years old, an age where she is exploring her world and testing her relationship with everything, she may feel that she killed him or was somehow responsible for his leaving. She will take the event personally, feeling that she must be at fault. If she does not think she magically killed him with some angry thought, then she might believe that her love was not enough to keep him alive. She may believe that she could have kept him alive with love if she were good enough, out of the mistaken idea that love heals all wounds and solves all problems. "He's gone and it's my fault."

Addicted to Control

We would rather be evil than powerless. We chose this as children to secure ourselves in the world. We would rather feel guilty because we caused the death of our parent than admit that we had no control over it. We fear helplessness because we feel that, if something happened to us once, it could happen to us again. But if we are responsible for events, even the death of a parent, then at least we have the power to avoid pain in the future. We sacrifice our basic goodness to our need for control and power. We develop an addiction to control rather than an openness to flow. We keep trying to obtain the power to control events.

Guilt and Shame as a Play for Power

Among the tools of power in this realm are guilt and shame. These portray our failures and painful experiences as unnecessary, as if we could have made things significantly different. We treat ourselves as if we had power that we never really had. It is important to realize, however, that if we *did* have the power at the time, we *would* have changed the event. We did not cause nor subconsciously choose the abusive and painful events of our lives. Again and again, the world was and is beyond our control.

We would even like to plan our own liberation. But life does not consult us. Everything else shows up in our life, and this is what is on our plate. We can only work with whatever is there—this is the plan. We would like it to be the reverse; we would like to control the plan and have everything else fit into our plan.

The irony for us as control addicts is that we are trying to be responsible for things that we cannot control, and we do not take responsibility for the things we can.

In the hell realm we continually assert the authority of our judgment and righteousness. When we are unsuccessful in determining an outcome, we are at least sure that we are "right." Exuding this type of energy creates tension in our relationships, giving others the choice of placating us, ignoring us, or resisting us. In each case there is no real spaciousness or authenticity. We either mistake genuine support for criticism or resist it as an attack on who we think we really are.

Victim as Victimizer

We project the inner tyranny of our anger into the world as we attempt to tyrannize each potentially threatening situation by displaying our sense of having been victimized and our righteousness. We perpetuate the process of victimization by making others victims, subjecting them to our judgments and our anger. Further, because our positions are so tied to righteousness, we mistake agreement for support and disagreement for opposition. We present our victim's view of the world with missionary zeal, and seek to convert others through the power of our pain and the evangelical demand that others recognize their own victimization.

Trapped in Victim Mentality

Hell thrives on double-binds, on ways of thinking that keep us trapped in our mindset. In this realm, criticism represents further victimization and is perceived as a form of aggression, thereby short-circuiting the possibility of observing the process and stopping it. Being caught in hell is further confirmation of how bad we are. Everything is filtered through the righteous, aggressive judgment of self and others. Every observation generates a win/loss type of judgment that in turn engenders resistance and counter-aggression.

All this results in loneliness, a lack of real connection. So we fall into depression, or we generate conflict in order to feel real and connected again.

In the hell realm, life is a constant struggle, an apparently never-ending fight to exist and to be okay. For some, this means swinging between intense hatred and aggression and a dull, exhausted resignation to the pain of existence, while still wishing for escape, possibly through suicidal acts of desperation.

The key phrases of the realm might be: "Life is unfair...," "Why me...?" "It was their fault...," "There must be something wrong with me...," "There must be something wrong with you or you wouldn't do this to me...," "I hate...," "Because of me...," "I resent...," "Should have..."

Before we can develop real insight into our habits of mind in this realm, we need to ask, "Is there a part of me that is dedicated to making sure that my life goes badly, because that would explain the pain, explain my situation? Is there a part that takes comfort in punishment?" The punishment could be providing the assurance that underneath all the wrongness and the failures, there is something worth saving. There is something right about us.

Resisting Becoming

Hell is created out of the resistance to "becoming" in an effort to solidify a sense of "being." The attempt to separate being from becoming, to deny the reality of change, alienates us from the nature of existence and makes us struggle against the flow of life. The effort to establish a permanent identity cuts us off from the very essence of aliveness—being fully present in the moment, undistracted by the past or the future, or by self-images.

What if there is no answer to the problem of our lives because there is no problem? What if the problem is invented, is only a projection? Suppose we are walking around in the world afraid of snakes. As we journey through snake country at dusk, every long thin shadow triggers our snake "radar" and places us on alert. In fact, our fear and caution would make us run or strike out rather than examine the evidence. This type of misperception creates a body response, in which the reality of the body's reaction overwhelms whatever is actually occurring at the time. The reaction becomes a reality unto itself, at least for a few moments.

This is similar to one of the Sufi stories of Nasrudin. Nasrudin goes to the doctor and is sitting outside the office with other patients waiting their turn. He keeps repeating the phrase, "I only hope I'm really sick." After listening to Nasrudin moan this phrase again and again, a patient finally asks him, "Why do you hope you are really sick?" Nasrudin looks helplessly at the other patients and says, "If I feel this bad, I only hope I'm really sick. I hate to think that anyone who feels as terrible as I do might be healthy."

Pretensions of Pain

We need to examine the nature of pain. What makes it so painful, aside from the fact that it hurts? What is the difference between pain and suffering? How does pain become suffering?

Blood clots and then stops flowing. Similarly, pain congeals into suffering. We prevent it from passing with our fear, hope, expectation, frustration, anxiety, blame, guilt, and shame. We become extra-sensitive, thinking that every sensation might be the beginning of more pain, thereby painfully bracing ourselves against the pain that might happen. We split ourselves between our desire for control and our ignorance of what is coming. We try to be prepared, "pre-tensing" to the point that we cannot move. Each "what if," "why," "how bad can it get," and "you did this to me" keeps the pain from fading into the past. We extend the pain as suffering.

Betraying Life

By identifying with the role of the victim and relating to life as a problem, we betray life in many ways. Part of us knows how to be alive in the moment, but we betray that part by putting all our attention on our story, our reconstruction of our life history. Our identity does not allow us to relate to the present as it really is. We stubbornly see ourselves as a victim, again, rather than as the author of our experience, now.

Spiritual Masquerade of the Penitent

Hell realm perspectives and habits also distort our approach to spirituality. We may think of ourselves as unworthy and appeal to the Divine to forgive us. We separate ourselves from the Divine, seeking purification from our sins. We may perform elaborate and painful vigils, fasts, and rituals, including physical or mental self-flagellation. We seek a teacher who is perfect to whom we can confess our failings. We want him or her to validate our suffering and to redeem us from our painful past. We are judgmental of the teacher's shortcomings and the failures of other students, particularly those who do not practice confession and purification. We may see our spiritual work as a battle for good against the evil forces in ourselves and the world. We may also limit ourselves by using meditation only as a device to control our pain and to provide us with temporary escapes into joy and peak experiences.

Suffering Builds Stamina

In hell we maintain the struggle while perpetuating the pain. As a result, we develop stamina. When not in the exhausted phase of the realm, we can marshall enormous energy by pursuing our point of view and telling our story. But there is also the potential here for reflection, if only we would create a pause from the chaos of our feelings and the tyranny of our righteousness.

Facing Our Addiction to Bad Feelings

We need to face our addiction to feelings such as shame, anger, and guilt. We need to deal with the ways in which we use pain to feel real. Attachment to the drama of the emotions needs to be confronted and penetrated before we can relax into the flow of life as it is.

Victim of Responsibility

Another barrier that must be overcome is our preoccupation with determining the origin and "cause" of suffering in order to place blame and act self-righteous. The "real cause" can never be determined. We are the way we are only partly because of our parents, who were somewhat the products of their parents, who grew up with their parents, and so on. Other factors may include the beliefs we formed from anomalous experiences, the influences of long-gone friends and acquaintances, and not getting enough sleep last night. It is much easier to stop the suffering now by interrupting the patterns than it is to find a real cause. We can take charge of now; we cannot do anything about the past. We can use our experience as the beginning of wisdom rather than as a continuation of ignorance.

Responsibility means the ability to respond. It is a matter of staying on course, meeting situations with our resources. We cannot be responsible for the world. To be responsible for the world is to become a victim of responsibility. As the therapist Yetta Bernhardt says, "To compete with God is one hell of a stress."

Changing Viewpoints

When we decide that the tradition of suffering in our family stops with us, then the suffering can be interrupted by a shift of viewpoints. It is a matter of relating to the process of becoming, to the flow of being, in a different way. We then look at life, see the flow of forces in life, and ask "How can these be used?" It is not a matter of changing one thing into something else, it is a matter of use. It is not a matter of what changes but of who changes. Samsara (the vicious cycle of reactive suffering that is created and perpetuated by the three poisons of ignorance, aggression and neediness) and Nirvana (the state beyond our self-images which are maintained by our vanity and by the three poisons) occur at the same address, everything depends on who is at home.

Flow as a Dynamic of Aliveness

The continuous flow of energy and changing phenomena is a part of what defines aliveness. Being awake and open to the freshness of each moment, feeling the energy of flowing with the course of events like a surfer riding a wave, and sensing the indestructible quality of awareness that encompasses all events and phenomena and reflects them all without being affected—these are the qualities that are obscured by our addiction to control, hostility, and righteousness. But we can confront the reality of life honestly and without contrivance, making our very awareness of our present condition the path to our freedom.

Acknowledging our weaknesses and our limited ability to affect events can be an important source of strength. From the viewpoint of spiritual warriorship, we hold our weaknesses in front of us so that they remain in our awareness. This fosters our honesty and forgiveness.

Forgiveness

Forgiveness includes a sense that we are bringing things to life again, to honesty. We are not going to carry the burden of vengeance. Vengeance keeps us locked into a victim stance, causing damage to ourselves or to someone else. Giving up this alleged right to cause pain is the beginning of an honest aliveness. We forgive ourselves, forgive whomever we feel victimized by, forgive God, and forgive the universe.

The desire for vengeance keeps us imprisoned. The difference between being a jailer and being a convict is simply which side of the bars we are on. When we desire vengeance, we are on both sides. When "parts of us" are punishing other "parts of us," our internal resources are fragmented. This reinforces the helplessness of our despair. Forgiveness releases both the convict and the jailer and heals the fragmentation.

Gratitude

Eventually this gives rise to gratitude, an advanced form of forgiveness. With gratitude, the heart opens and spiritual life begins. Without gratitude, there is no spiritual development, only empty gestures. When we have heartfelt gratitude for the miracle of our existence, the gift of life, then we have enough, and everything else becomes an extra gift. Then we can appreciate and marvel at the wonder of life. Through forgiveness, gratitude, appreciation, and the sense of being enough, the flow of life becomes an opportunity rather than a threat. There is no need to block the flow of life, no need to prove something, and no need to ignore anything. There develops an appreciation of the process of manifestation and a patience with the unfolding nature of life.

Patience in Action

The process by which we grow spiritually involves surrendering to the flow, allowing the universal to operate through us, and integrating that into our being. Within the flow of change, there is something that can be relied on. When we realize this, a serene, peaceful patience develops.

We may experience a form of this patience within activity at times when we consciously—without being self-conscious or mechanical—are fully engaged in a demanding or exciting activity. The sense of flow, of immediate sensations, and of undistracted openness can be felt when skillfully shooting the rapids in a kayak, effortlessly skiing down a steep slope, or passionately making love. When we become the activity, feeling connected to each moment, to each event, we are no longer alienated from life. In that instant, we are not waiting for something else to happen. Our longing for love as a way out of separateness is dissolved in our belonging to the present.

With no waiting, no holding back, we open to activity and change. We meet whatever life presents and dance with it. We trust the flows that make up our being, are a part of our becoming, and provide the vitality and stamina that sustains us from moment to moment.

Ramana Maharshi spoke about people riding on a train. Seeing the scenery passing by so quickly, they fear they may lose their luggage. They grab their belongings and hold them tightly on top of their heads, afraid that something from the passing scenery could take their luggage. Eventually, they realize that they are moving and the scenery is relatively still. They realize that that which is moving them is also moving their luggage and they place what is theirs on the seat beside them. What is ours goes along with us. There is no need for an extra effort to hang on to what or who we are.

Unperturbability

As we come to realize the ease of being who we are, we develop the natural curiosity of unperturbable awareness as our way of encountering life and the world moment to moment. Unperturbable awareness is not a passive stolid state; it meets each new situation with intense, active interest in a way that cannot be distracted or disturbed. "Who and what we are" is a journey of discovery into each new moment. This awareness in turn gives rise to mirror-like wisdom. Our Essence nature is mirror-like, reflecting all yet remaining the same no matter what is reflected.

The great mirror of awareness reflects both content—objects and experiences—and emptiness. Here "emptiness" means that content is empty of inherent existence. No object, behavior, phenomenon, thought, or feeling has the inherent reality that we habitually give it when we see things as having solid existence. It has no nature of its own apart from every-thing else and from our perception of it. Our realization of unperturbable awareness leads to the recognition of the essen-tially empty nature of reality and frees us from living as if all our assumptions and ideas were true.

Perceiving the world as devoid of inherent existence can purify our attachments and habits of mind. This realization is a cleansing process and an emotional bath. Yet, with this awareness, we do not get lost in some vast abstract space. As Lama Govinda says, it "reveals the 'emptiness' in the things as much as the things in the 'emptiness'." It is not enough to realize the universal, the infinite, Essence. We must realize the universal through our individual existence and thus realize Essence in life.

These realizations free us from our habitual preoccupa-tions so that we have nothing to prove, nothing to fear, and nothing to hide. We no longer need to hide ourselves from the world or to hide the world from ourselves. By operating unat-tached to and freed from our agendas of vanity and insecurity, we no longer obscure the nature of grace, the gift of life as it is. We flow with the process of becoming and living. We host experience and life situations with interest, involvement and gratitude.

Meditation

Two types of meditation are particularly useful in reveal-ing the dynamics of aliveness and developing the wisdom qualities from the contraction of the hell realm. The first is analytical and inquiry meditations, especially meditations that center around the nature of phenomena, of process, and of emptiness. The second is energetic practices that balance and expand the energies of the body, particularly the emotions, so we can use them to cultivate our qualities of aliveness and radiate those qualities to others.

Analytical Meditation

When doing analytical meditation, we seek to reveal our patterns of thought and feeling as they are, to examine and clarify the basic nature of reality, to discover the process of thought arising, and to come to a direct recognition of the nature of Essence and the inherent emptiness of all phenomena. This eventually brings a direct, intuitive knowing that frees us from the tyranny of habitual thinking, feeling, and behaving.

During analytical meditation we use our conceptual capacity to engage in an intensive process of investigation. Unlike our everyday thinking in which we are bombarded by stimuli and react to situations, during meditation sessions we are able to concentrate and to develop greater sensitivity to the workings of our minds.

Begin the meditation by placing your attention on your palm or breath, letting your body and mind ease into the process until you feel relaxed and alert. You may also want to expand your inner smile throughout your body. Being in touch with your purpose and desire to become free through your meditation, reflect on the benefits that will come to you and others from this process.

Make mental notes of the thoughts that arise, labeling them and then letting them pass, such as "hearing a bird," "feeling sad," "feeling angry," "thinking about my pain." The arising, noting, and passing of each thought and feeling is used as a reminder of the impermanent nature of phenomena.

When you are able to do this comfortably, shift the focus of attention to the thinker in you. Maintain your attention on the process of thought and note insights into the nature of the mind.

Now, methodically and carefully become aware of the I. Who or what is thinking, feeling, and meditating? How does it exist? Can it be located? Is it your body? Is it in a part of your body? Explore every part of the body, even the organs and cells, in an effort to discover where you might find your I. Is your I the mind? A creation of the mind? Does it exist concretely and independently in its own right?

Then mentally disintegrate your body, imagining all the cells and atoms dissolving and floating away, like sugar dissolving in water. Imagine that you can see all of the particles that were your body spread out over the entire vastness of space. Now do the same with the mind, dissolving and scattering all thoughts, feelings, attitudes, sensations, and perceptions.

Remain in this experience of space. When a self-sense arises again, repeat the process of analysis. As Kathleen McDonald warns, "Do not make the mistake of thinking, 'My body is not the I and my mind is not the I, therefore I don't exist.' You *do* exist, but not in the way you instinctively feel, that is as independent and inherent. Conventionally, your self exists *in dependence upon* mind and body, and this combination is the basis to which conceptual thinking ascribes a name: 'I' or 'self' or 'Mary' or 'Harold.' This is the you that is sitting and meditating and wondering, 'Maybe I don't exist!'"

Finish the meditation with the realization that this is one step along the way of cutting through the roots of suffering. Note the insights gained and the supportive energies generated and radiate those out to others and the world.

Another way you can use this process of inquiry is to make the question the subject of the meditation. Instead of seeking answers to the question of your inquiry, maintain your attention on the question itself. The mind, in its habitual way, cannot seem to stop seeking answers. First one answer comes, then another, and possibly even the thought that there is no answer, and that is an answer as well. You may find yourself continually trying to provide an adequate response to the question.

One of the experiences that can occur in this process is a pause. Whether out of frustration or simple relaxation, a break in your mental habits occurs. Then you can simply be with the question, be with the flow and the openness of the experience of the question without trying to solidify any particular position.

Orbiting and Balancing Energies

The second type of meditation continues the process of using your attention to purify and develop your energy. After placing attention and recalling your purpose for meditating, imagine drawing in breath and energy through your forehead and moving the energy down through the energy centers in the front of your body on the inhalation and releasing the energy up the back with the exhalation. Place the tongue at the roof of the mouth so that the energy can flow easily from the forehead to the throat. As the energy passes through each of the centers in the body—the forehead, the throat, the heart, the solar plexus, the navel, the sexual center, the root at the perineum, the coccyx, the sacrum, the center on the back opposite the navel, the center opposite the solar plexus, the center opposite the heart center, the center opposite the throat, the center between the top of the spine and the base of the skull, and finally the center at the crown of the head—imagine that each of them is activated, balanced, and expanded.

In this process your imagination will lead to sensations and the sensations to realization of the energy flows and patterns. After the energy reaches the crown center, some of it can be released out through the top of the head and some brought down the front to mix with the energies being drawn in through the center in the forehead. This orbit keeps the energy

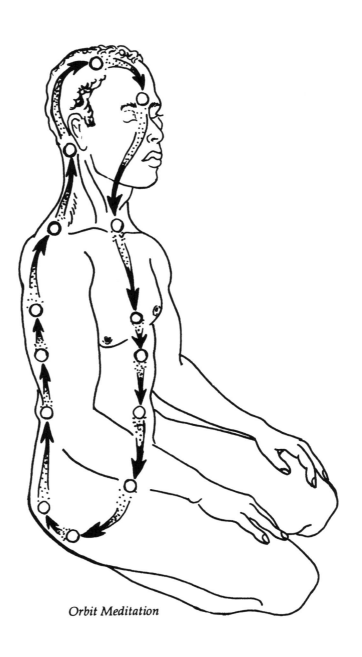

Orbit Meditation

flowing and prevents it from getting stuck in a particular center in the body. It also creates a balance within and between the energy centers. You may also imagine that you are drawing down the energy of the heavens with your inhalation and drawing up the energies of the earth with your exhalation, thus maintaining a balance between the two and experiencing your-self as a connection between them.

A variation that opens and expands each of the energy centers, or chakras, involves conscious breathing. Breathe into a selected center (it is best to begin with the center in the forehead) as if you are smelling a rose, enjoying the odor and absorbing the wonderful sensation of it into your body. Hold the breath, as if to savor it, relaxing and letting the sensation saturate the center and expand it. Each time you draw in your breath to the chakra, the energy will have the chance to expand and penetrate deeper. As you release the breath, tensions and resistances can flow out, creating a greater sense of freedom.

Vitality of Patience

In the hell realm attitude, we are angry at the pain of loneliness and separation. We can escape our inner isolation by intentionally going deeper into our inner world with our analytical scalpel and surgically revealing the emptiness of our identities, preoccupations, and stories. When we also release the blockages of energies so that they flow freely, we feel the vitality and connection of each immediate moment. Patience is not a state of frustrated waiting, but a feeling of being complete in each moment.

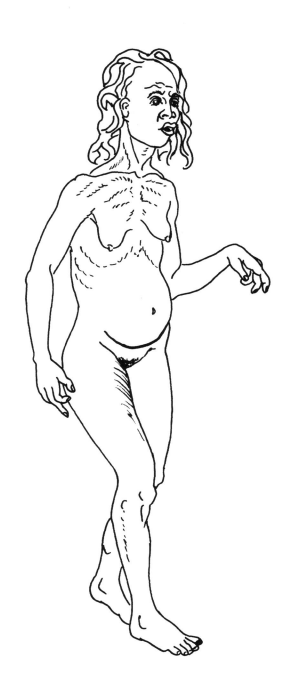

6

If Only:
When Enough is Not Enough

The Hungry Ghost Realm and the
Generation of Value

Eeyore, the old grey donkey, stood by the side of the
stream, and looked at himself in the water.
"Pathetic," he said. "That's what it is. Pathetic."
A.A. Milne, Winnie the Pooh

Footfalls in the memory
Down the passage which we did not take
Towards the door we never opened
Into the rose-garden.
T. S. Eliot, Burnt Norton

Work is love made visible.
Kahlil Gibran, The Prophet

*The realm of the pretas or hungry ghosts is occupied by beings
who have large mouths, big eyes, long, very thin necks, shrivelled
limbs, and huge bellies. They are always hungry and continually
devouring whatever seems likely to fulfill their insatiable appetites.*

But there is never enough. They always feel that if only the missing pieces of their lives were there, then they would be happy.

Their attachment to desire turns water into fire. Every time they try to quench their thirst, they not only fail to satisfy their desires, but because the water turns into fire, they only feel the need of it more.

Avalokiteshvara appears as his Spiritual Father Amitabha and as the Divine Mother Pandaravasini. Amitabha is red like the setting sun. His hands rest in his lap in a meditative pose, with a fully opened lotus of unfolding, creative meditation upon his hands. From his heart radiates the deep red light of discriminating wisdom. He sits on a peacock throne. Pandaravasini, his consort, is also red but wears a white robe, representing her stainless nature. Amitabha projects a warming and comforting kind of presence while conveying the capacity for distinction-making perception to the indiscriminate and insatiable beings. Pandaravasini sees their real nature and coaxes it out with her magnetic presence. In combination, they seem to the pretas as though they can fulfill any and every desire and need.

The divine couple hand each preta a radiant, priceless jewel, instructing each one to pass it on to someone else, shifting his gaze from the jewel to the face of the receiver. The preta thus possesses the jewel just long enough to appreciate the preciousness of the gift before he passes that gift on to someone else, who in turn does the same. In this way, each preta appreciates the qualities of the jewels, thereby developing the capacity for discrimination. Each passes on that value to others, thus developing the wisdom of generosity, realizing that greater value flows to them from the act of giving than anything they might have received from the object itself.

"I DON'T FEEL LOVABLE, so who would be interested in me? I'm stuck in a low-paying teaching job that is fine in terms of the kids, but it's not what I want. I'm not good enough at my music and not motivated enough to make things happen outside my teaching job. I'm too scared that people won't like my music. It was better when I was younger. I was married and felt I was beginning a career. Now, everyone I know is doing something more important, more exciting, and more respected than I am. I'm divorced and my friends are married. Sure I have a nice home and some guaranteed income from alimony and child support, but I can't travel like my friends or buy a really nice car, or furnish my house the way I want. I feel empty and lonely because no one is interested in marrying someone who is slightly neurotic, middle-aged, only moderately attractive and has kids." These complaints of a workshop participant are typical of those of us who look with hopeless distress at what is missing from our lives.

Preoccupied with Not Enough

The "preta," or hungry ghost, realm is a state of mind preoccupied with not being enough, a deep sense of inadequacy. As inhabitants of this realm, we have insatiable desire; we perceive self, others, the world, the present, and the past in terms of comparative evaluations; we approach experience and situations as opportunities to consume; and we think that the source of our inadequacy and dissatisfaction is rooted in the past.

In this realm we relate to what is missing, to what has been lost, to an idealized past, and to a fantasized future. Our core concern is to fill an inner void and prevent physical and emotional emptiness from overwhelming us. If only we could achieve satisfaction, if only we could gain a sense of meaning and worth, we could permanently fill this inner void. In this struggle we are dissatisfied with the present, and we ignore the value of what is here now.

When we feel fundamentally impoverished, the discrepancy between what we are and what we would like to be seems like a negative judgment. We may yearn for a past when things were better, or look to some ideal future that seems out of reach. No matter how we try to measure or validate our worth, competence, and life situations, we are never enough. Our appetite for what we want—friendship, ideas, information, money, power, respect, food, sex—always exceeds what we currently have or what we could possibly maintain.

Constantly Hungry

As hungry ghosts, we want to devour life, hoping that in this way we will feel more substantial. We are constantly hungry for some new experience that might satisfy our emptiness. Unfulfilled, we then see life as an obstacle to our getting what we feel we need. The pain of frustrated wanting is amplified when we realize that we cannot get what we want. This, in turn, intensifies our sense of inadequacy, which only fuels our voracious hunger.

Even when we fill ourselves with something we want, we tend to rush through the process in our desire to overcome the pain of wanting, and so we miss the experience, like chugging a bottle of fine wine. The frustration of missing the taste propels us to consume even more. Finally, uncomfortably bloated from overdoing it, we regret having senselessly skipped the pleasure.

We swing between the struggle to satisfy desires and the frustration of getting what we thought we wanted. The operating force here is hunger—the constant desire for whatever is not there. We hunger for relief from the constant sense of hunger and incompleteness.

In this realm, we imagine all the wonderful things that used to be in our life or that could or should be in our life now. We fantasize an oasis of riches while struggling in our desert of "now." We envision delicious fruit and are disappointed to find it has a worm or that the good fruit is too expensive. We frequently fantasize about the possibility of satisfying our desires, go for it, and are disappointed that it didn't work out or was not what we expected.

Seeking Relief in Dreams

We are undeterred by disappointment, because all we know how to do is dream of other possibilities for relief. So we keep pursuing our fantasy dreams, whether to recapture an idealized past or to plan for an imagined future, and keep wishing that somehow things would work out.

One result of this relentless pursuit is a love-hate relationship with our dreams. Instead of using dreams to inspire creative action toward our goals, we make them into untouchable gods with power over our lives. We are attracted to their glamour, yet repelled by the disappointment and frustration they bring. We feel some ease as we mentally enact the dreams, but when we seek to realize them, we encounter the inevitable pain of dissatisfaction.

This pain of dissatisfaction allows us to feel real. We may even elevate dissatisfaction to an ideal because it motivates us toward action and achievement. Our theme song is *"not enough"*—not enough life, not enough richness, not enough excitement, not enough accomplishments, not enough experiences, not enough pleasure, not enough challenges. There is not enough of whatever would make us feel whole, adequate, and worthwhile.

The hunger and pain of dissatisfaction and the dream of satisfaction all provide us with something to relate to, something that can make us feel that we exist and have a task in the world. Our quest in this realm is for a lost Garden of Eden where everything was provided for us, where we felt complete and at one with the universe.

Loss and Deprivation

The wound in this realm is a sense of loss and deprivation. We explain our inner hunger by looking at our past and focusing on what was taken away or how we were abandoned. We generate elaborate theories about the perfect childhood we did not have. We feel that our childhood needs were not met and must be satisfied before we can be complete.

A popular approach to healing our neediness employs the concept of the "inner child," a personification of the wounded part of us. As a metaphor for fixations on needs and desires, this approach can be useful for exploring our developmental patterns and working through emotional issues, if it results in resolution. But as an organizing principle or context for our relationships, or as a way of feeling real, it distracts us from the present, fragments us, and prevents us from growing up. Living our lives to please the inner child is like living our lives to please Santa Claus. Although expedient at a certain period of our life, as an ongoing reality it does not allow us to mature and parent ourselves. Thus we need to beware of turning a tool for growth into yet another fixation of the realm.

Pursuing Pity

Fearing loneliness in our struggle to be enough and have enough, we seek pity. Pity is the agreement from others, or from some part of ourselves, that our situation is sorrowful, worthy of the sense of deprivation and grief. We use pity to validate our longing and our quest to prove that we are sufficient. We use pity to feel connection and belonging, even though it is through the "deformity" of our inadequacy. We sell out our aliveness in the present to obtain pity for our history of loss.

As we adopt an attitude of self-pity, we often create alliances with others who feel similarly, thus forming relationships of mutual validation. Through symbiotic relationships of sympathetic attention, we "nourish" each other with emotionally gory stories of unfulfilled needs, abandonment, violation, disappointment and dreams of salvation.

As pretas, we may use support groups to feed our self-pity rather than to foster relationships that can help us grow beyond pain into maturity, autonomy, and our basic capacity for creating value. We change steps into stops as a way of clinging to our preta identity.

Comparing and Regretting

As hungry ghosts, our constant comparisons amplify our sense of deprivation and inadequacy. We compare the present with the past; the present with our ideas about what should be; the past with what should have been; ourselves to others; and what is with what might have been. "How does this fall short (of what it should be)?" "How am I less (than what I could have been)?"

We pay attention to what we are not getting, rather than to what we are giving. We define satisfaction in terms of what we have and consume rather than what we create and produce. We live in a world of what might have been, ignoring what is. We see only the roads not taken rather than those that still lie before us. Our values become needs rather than energizers of the soul and foundations for sharing. We relate to goals as indicators of failure rather than as guides and treat feedback as the proof of error. Our life becomes stuck in what used to make a difference rather than what matters now, and we dwell on how the past limits our future, rather than opening to our present aliveness.

By looking at the present in terms of the past that did happen, as well as the past that did not happen but should have, we say "if only" to life and engender regret. Regret extends frustration and disappointment by fixing them in our memory and making them part of our personal history. We nourish a pervasive sense of distress and longing that always lurks in the background of our actions and emotions.

With these "if"s we place living into a conditional frame of reference. Our life, happiness, aliveness, relationships, and actions are conditioned by our comparisons, evaluations, and regrets. Our estimations of what we can be, what we can become, and what we can share are determined by our "sacred" past. Our judgments of what should have been and should be plague us in the present moment. We hold immediate experience hostage until our longing can be satisfied and our regrets dissolved.

Heart Posture of "Not Being Enough" and Regret

Even when we get our act together and things start to work out for us, we will sabotage the present with our "if"s. We succeed in snatching defeat from the jaws of victory. This happens because our posture of the heart is that "we are not enough," and we scan our experiences and successes until we find how things fall short. Since we consider disappointment and regret to be real, we push situations until we experience disappointment and regret. Only then are we sure of the truth.

Comfort of Familiarity

Painful and ineffective behaviors feel real because they are familiar. This familiarity conveys a false sense of solidity, a sense that something in us persists over time. As we repeat behaviors, they become easier and more comfortable. These actions no longer require any effort of decision or implementation. We derive comfort from this ease even though the results may be painful and disappointing. In this way ineffective behaviors are reinforced and become habits. Our habits, seeming to persist over time, placate our desire for a permanent identity.

We become addicted to familiar behaviors and the objects that they attempt to secure. The nature of addiction is that we can never get enough of what we don't really want—but we think we can. The heart posture in addiction is "almost." It seems that a little bit more of "almost" would be "it." Even more "almost" will definitely be "it." However, "it" always ends up as "almost."

When we are thirsty, if we eat potato chips it "almost" quenches our thirst. Then we eat bag after bag of potato chips, eating perhaps two or three bags only because we do not have five bags. But the salt dehydrates us, leaving us even more thirsty. More thirst, more salt; more salt, more thirst. Similarly, more habit, fewer results; fewer results, more habit.

Missing Life and Pretending We're Not

These cycles wound us and distract us. We miss the living experience of now as we pay attention to the melodrama of our inner world. We are not giving life to our aliveness, but to our sense of need, our hunger. Something inside knows that we are missing life itself.

A real spiritual pain in our soul is evoked constantly by this process of ignoring the living moment. If our story is dramatic enough, the spiritual pain is dulled somewhat by distraction. However, blocking awareness never cures anything. People usually fall asleep just before they freeze to death.

Our body and soul know that the mind is not attending to "what is," and is instead directing our attention and energy to stories. We are playing "let's pretend." Let's pretend that the past is true "now." Let's pretend that our regrets are real and justified. Let's organize ourselves in such a way as to make our pretense seem real, so real, in fact, that we are not sure anything else is real.

Our pretenses are a distortion of who we are. Literally, we "pre-tense"; we create tension prior to events in order to control and maintain our imagined reality. These distortions are a constant wound that can be healed in an instant by being present with "what is," without conditions, agendas, or considerations. Until that happens, we experience the pain of contraction of our soul, and we think this pain is really our unsatisfied hunger. We attempt to cope with a spiritual pain by interpreting it as an emotional or physical phenomenon. In addition, we fear the openness through which real creation takes place because we interpret it as a threat to our existence and feeling of being real.

In the preta realm, everything is defined in terms of comparisons. Experience of "what is" is stolen by the constant comparison to what it is not. We become a ghost to life because, instead of living life now as it is, we haunt every experience with comparisons, all the while hungering for the experience. In this way, the hungry ghost continues to starve in the midst of plenty. We divorce ourselves from life and fall into suffering, a situation that is familiar and appears controllable, if not satisfying and alive. Each experience then becomes a stimulus for retreating once more into the conviction that we are always deprived of satisfying experience.

Wanting to Satisfy Insatiable Desires

As pretas, we are caught in the double-bind of thinking that satisfaction and meaning can be achieved through the fulfillment of desires that cannot be fulfilled. Tensing in this way, we push ourselves further into fantasizing how life used to be, must have been, should have been, could be, or should be.

In addition, we cling to our painful habits as something familiar, while hoping that change will end our suffering. We want immortality for our identity and mortality for our pain. We try to perpetuate the self that feels painfully real, and to eliminate the pain that validates our existence and gives meaning to our life. We are trapped between our fear of the pain of wanting and the fear that we may not exist or that life may be meaningless.

Reducing the World to Commodities

When we try to establish the reality of our own existence, we treat experiences, ourselves, others, and the world as things to consume. We essentially reduce them all to data and objects. We want information so we can evaluate how things serve our needs and what it will take to get them. Everything becomes a commodity. By reducing each thing to the amount of satisfaction it might give us, we deaden ourselves to the unique qualities that make things individual and distinct. We not only ignore the richness of life and other people, but we try to hide from our fear of their unknown qualities.

Spiritual Masquerade of the Humble Seeker

As pretas, we often search for the spiritual experience that will fill the hole inside. We sample workshops, take retreats, and get empowerments from many teachers. We think that if we consume enough from the smorgasbord of the spiritual marketplace we will feel complete and peaceful. We want a teacher who will meet our needs. Although we sense that our neediness comes from a deep spiritual hunger, we buy what makes us feel better and discard what is confusing and unfamiliar. We think: "If only I had the right teacher. If only I had started earlier. If only I had learned how to be disciplined when I was a child. Then I would be a master. Then I could practice compassion. Then I could be peaceful and happy."

We feel inadequate for spiritual work and defeated by comparison with the teacher and other serious students. The teacher seems remote and inaccessible, and the teachings seem too expensive and time-consuming. We act humble out of a sense of self-defeat rather than out of gratitude for the teachings and wonder at the richness of life.

Creating Value

The feelings of loss, disappointment, hunger, and regret all reflect our desire for something that is missing, for a greater richness. Richness is also the basis for the natural dynamic of value generation underlying this realm. As infants we openly gave and received. Even in our receiving there was a generosity of presence. The concern with consuming emerged when we were encouraged to define what we wanted, and to give attention to "what is missing."

Behind every need is a value, something that is worth manifesting in the world. What is important is not the thing we think will satisfy the value but the value itself. The value is worth having because it improves the quality of life. From this point of view, the value of transporting people is more important than the ownership of a car. Creating a pleasing environment for interacting with other people is more important than being attractive.

Value is to the spirit what air is to the lungs. Every behavior has a value underlying it, even if the behavior itself is a distorted means to achieve that value. We are continually trying to achieve something of worth, even though we may be using archaic or ineffective means to reach our goals.

Into the Unknown

Surprise is one way to escape these familiar ruts. Surprise interrupts our patterns of hunger, control, and expectation. It is a principal ingredient in the experiences of delight and humor. It opens us to the unknown, the "not knowing" way of being.

When we don't know and can relax the tension of "should know," "not knowing" can be a natural openness in which we become more aware. Within this open awareness, we see the radiance and connection of all beings and phenomena. We move beyond our inner world of deprivation and isolation.

This awareness is not a form of logical thought, but of clear, intuitive vision. Vision is possible when we meditate in a way that frees our consciousness from agendas, preconceptions, and presumed knowledge.

The ability to meditate with openness takes discipline, time, and self-awareness. In meditation we often repeat the patterns of the rest of our lives. We approach meditation with goals and agendas and ideas about what can and should be achieved. These become our spiritual dreams, upon which we skewer our practice by comparison. If we let this process continue, meditation becomes stale and potentially a source of additional preta suffering.

The Key to Meditation

The key to freshness in meditation is relaxing into "not knowing." Notice the goals and ideas that are there. Realize that they, too, are part of the apparatus of illusion and fantasy. Acknowledge that we do not know what we are doing or who is doing it. And open to what is actually occurring at the time. The unknown is always present, but it is obscured by our knowledge, our concepts and our filters of perception. Releasing these mental constructs allows a more direct knowing to occur, one that is freed from dualities and ideas.

Boundless Radiance

The boundless radiance of each moment provides the light for seeing with clarity. From this intuitive vision comes awareness of the value inherent in each experience. We embrace giving as a natural aspect of aliveness. The boundless light reveals the boundless nature of life, the endless and pervasive aliveness of each moment.

We have glimpses of this boundless radiance when our romantic love is first fulfilled. Suddenly our joy knows no bounds and the entire world comes alive. Luminous energy shines from our heart, lighting up the universe. Every color is vivid, every line is distinct. And every sound is musical. The moment is eternal. The experience is beyond our concepts, beyond our imagination. Our being feels higher and wider.

The openness derived from "not knowing" makes further steps toward freedom possible. In one sense, the way out of the hungry ghost realm is through openness and generosity. When we can go beyond the pressure to "know" and open ourselves to what is here now, our openness itself engages the present. This sense of presence engenders satisfaction and delight.

We then want to share this with others. The first gift that we have to offer is our attention. When we give our attention, it carries our energy and our intention.

The Path of Giving

Liberation from the preta realm into the realization of value generation and generosity involves the practice of giving. To give, we must first find something worth giving, something of value. We achieve this by directing our attention toward the richness of the world and of life. We view what is here and how bountiful life is, especially its possibilities and our own inner resources. Then, selecting among these resources, we pass them on to others. The self-preoccupation and self-pity of this realm begin to disintegrate as we give others the gift of our attention and our energy.

As we inquire into our own nature, we come to understand that our very being generates value. The fact that "we are" generates value. There is nothing special about it. Our nature inherently shows up and generates value. This value is beyond experience and yet includes what we value in experience.

The search for meaning is actually a desire to be in touch with our inherent worth. Our very presence contributes to making the world what it is, simply by us being who we are. This differs from utilitarian or relational values, which are conditional. Our presence is the worth of the Divine manifesting through us—our aliveness is a form of Divine affirmation and blessing. This inherent value is reflected in every being and in every being's relationship with everything else.

Thus our generosity grows out of the value we inherently create and out of our instinctive urge to share and to belong. Over time, our developing capacity for expression extends to more functional and relational domains by contributing something of worth to others.

Establishing the Ground for Awakening

Awakening into the natural dynamic qualities of our being and realizing the wisdom qualities of aliveness requires conscious work. Although enlightenment is a form of recognition and can happen in an instant, the ground needs to be prepared beforehand. We create the proper conditions by providing what is needed at each stage of the preparatory process, using awareness and energy practices. There are several stages in this process. The seeds need to be planted through initiation or transmission; there follows a dormant stage; then, through our practices, we cultivate the seeds and insure favorable conditions for growth; finally, after a growing period, our efforts can bear the fruit of realization.

We are working toward a realization of completeness. Once we acquire the intuitive understanding that we are parts of a whole and that each of us has the whole, or Essence, as our basis, we realize that we are a conscious expression of the whole. Then we can awaken into the reality of true freedom. In this way, understanding leads to realization, and realization leads to freedom.

As Lama Govinda put it:

> The Buddhist does not endeavor to "dissolve his being in the infinite," to fuse his finite consciousness with the consciousness of the all, or to unite his soul with the

all-soul; his aim is to become **conscious** of his ever-existing, indivisible and undivided completeness. To this completeness nothing can be added, and from it nothing can be taken away. It may only be experienced or recognized in a more or less perfect way.

The goal is not to expand our individual consciousness to the cosmic universal, but to realize that the universe becomes conscious in us individually. The dualistic concepts of self and other, individual and universal, inside and outside, part and whole, and "I" and "not-I," are all illusions. They have a functional usefulness depending on the context, but no inherent reality. From the viewpoint of completeness, true realization has all the elements of universality without presuming an external cosmos, and all the components of individual experience without presuming a separate entity or identity.

Our steady inquiry into the nature of our thoughts and feelings uses everything as a means toward our realization and our freedom. We understand that our needs and desires are manifestations of our thirst for life, which is realized through our aliveness in each moment.

Every person, every act, every process of becoming and disappearing, is an expression of a transcending reality that becomes conscious through each one of these phenomena. Thus the "contents" of everyday life resemble symbolic stories that reveal meanings beyond the specific people and events they describe.

Wisdom of Radiance and Generating Value

As we practice and grow, the clarity of our boundless radiance becomes a gift to all. Our ideal is the Buddhist concept of the "bodhisattva." Bodhisattvas are people who, in their own path to enlightenment, dedicate themselves to relieving the suffering of all sentient beings. "Bodhi" means the understanding or wisdom of the ultimate nature of reality, or Essence, and a "sattva" is someone who is an authentic being, motivated by true nature. Compassion is the expression of authentic being. The bodhisattva tries to combine infinite compassion with infinite wisdom. The bodhisattva path is the hero's journey of the awakening being. The archetype for this type of hero is Avalokiteshvara, someone whose heartache is greater than his or her headache, who reinvests his or her final liberation in others.

This journey depends on developing three dimensions of work. The first is self-reliance. We need to be able to take care of ourselves, and give appropriate attention to the physical, emotional, and spiritual aspects of our lives. Once we can care for ourselves, we can serve others, which becomes the second dimension. In this service to others, the boundaries of the self enlarge and become transparent, transmitting openness, relationship, patience, generosity of spirit, presence, and harmony. The third dimension concerns working with the energetic dance of the world. In traveling through these three dimensions, we are always working with self, other and world.

Spiritual work is the process of transforming the habit body—our habitual ways of thinking, feeling, and behaving—into a dedication body, so that our way of being and our actions are directed toward the benefit of others. Emulating the bodhisattva, we cultivate this dedication body as a gift to others, supporting them on the path of freedom, before we enter the void of the final liberation.

Meditating on the Suffering of Others

Three exercises can be useful in developing this dedication body. In the first, we meditate on suffering and compassion; in the second, drawn from the Hwa Yen School of China, we radiate virtues; and in the third, we receive the suffering of others, transform it, and send out radiance.

Begin by placing your attention and recalling your purpose. Visualize or sense that all beings are in the space around you and contemplate their suffering. Think of the suffering of your parents and of those close to you. Open your heart to their physical, psychological and emotional difficulties and realize that, like you, they wish to be free of all suffering. Experience how wonderful it would be if they were free and could feel peace and joy.

Repeat this process with acquaintances and people you may not like or get along with, realizing that they are governed by the same habitual patterns as you are, and open your heart to them. Extend this to all beings.

A variation on this exercise involves using a partner. Imagine a crystal in the middle of your heart center and place your attention there. Fill your entire being with the radiance of the crystal, sensing the radiance as light, as the vibration of sound, and as sensation. Radiate in all directions endlessly. Then receive the radiance of your partner with your inhalation. Send radiance to your partner on the exhalation. Extend the receiving and sending of radiance to others and to all beings. Sense the receiving and sending pulse. Finally, relax your effort and abide. End by dedicating your meditation to the benefit of all.

Radiating Virtues

The second exercise begins by accessing a series of virtuous qualities within yourself. When you feel your body and mind pervaded by the quality of a particular virtue, radiate it outward, filling all space with the radiance of that quality. The qualities to start with are:

A Great Compassionate Heart, that longs to protect all.

A Great Loving Heart, that longs to benefit all beings.

An Understanding Heart, that generates empathy and welcoming.

A Free Heart, that longs to remove obstructions from others.

A Heart that fills the universe.

A Heart Endless and Vast as Space.

A Pure Heart that is not limited by past, present, or future.

These qualities already exist within you; it is a matter of accessing them, amplifying their resonance, and radiating them to others.

Receiving and Sending

You can do a simple exercise of receiving and sending to further develop this feeling of relationship and compassion. Begin by picturing a black hole—so intense that not even light escapes its gravitational pull—in your heart. Thinking of something you are suffering from, consider that there are other beings who are suffering in a similar way. Sensing the black hole in your heart, breathe in your suffering and that of all beings. Realizing that, if it were possible, you would give your life to remove all the suffering in the world, hold that suffering in your heart. Feeling the pressure of your held breath and of your heart center breaking the suffering down into its essential energy, bring to mind a joy that has made your life worth living. Feel your heart being saturated with that joy. When you exhale, radiate that joy as a white light to the hearts of all other beings.

In this way you are making your heart center into a transformer and a generator of value. Your heart digests the energy of suffering and uses it as food for generating aliveness in yourself and others. Life becomes the gymnasium of the spirit, and you use everyday situations as an opportunity to exercise and develop your spiritual muscle.

As we open to our aliveness in this way and work through the habitual contractions of our soul, we need to be willing to undergo "heartbreak," in order to experience a kind of tenderness. We may experience a change of heart and then, as with other kinds of significant life changes, we lose something familiar. The solidity of our familiar identity and orientation toward what is real cracks and falls away, revealing our natural radiance and completeness.

7

Beyond Struggle and the Quest for Power
From Titan Realm to Skillful Means

Sure winning isn't everything. It's the only thing.
"Red" Sanders

Fanaticism consists in redoubling your effort when
you have forgotten your aim.
George Santayana, Life of Reason, Volume 1

Only where love and need are one
And the work is play for mortal stakes
Is the deed ever really done
For Heaven and the future's sakes.
Robert Frost, "Two Tramps in Mud Time"

The Titans, dressed in full armor, are beings inflamed by jealousy. They see everything in terms of struggle, feel attacked by the gods, and seek the power to become gods. A giant tree grows on the border between the titan realm and the god realm and bears wish-granting fruit. While the tree grows in the territory of the titans, the fruit falls in the land of the gods. The gods, oblivious of where the blessings come from, eat the fruit and toss the pits over the wall between the two realms, which the titans take to be arrows of assault. They fire arrows and spears toward the gods, which magically turn to blossoms as they descend into their neighbor's realm.

Avalokiteshvara appears to the titans as the Spiritual Father Amogasiddhi, realizer of the aim and of all-accomplishing wisdom, and as the Divine Mother Tara, the All-Merciful. Amogasiddhi is an impeccably skilled warrior who remains cool and fearless in the face of attacks by all the titans, and who radiates a luminous green light. Unable to defeat him, the titans attempt to learn his skill. As they learn to separate their actions from their emotions, and to develop the qualities of skillful means—stillness and quietude, freshness of being, cool unfettered mind, productive activity, harmony with both comrades and opponents, precision, and selfless volition—their original desire to conquer the kingdom of the gods is undermined by their realization that there is nothing to be gained by the struggle.

Tara, as a "savior," invites the titans, particularly the female titans, to look into the pool of tears they have shed for their husbands, brothers, and sons lost in battle. They reflect on the suffering that flows from their sense of entitlement, their tendency to be aggressive, and their orientation toward struggle. From this reflection comes a pause, a realization of the dangers of fixation, and a sense of grace and gratitude.

WHEN WE LIVE in the titan realm, we want to prove that we deserve to be respected, to be honored, to be loved, to be secure, and to be treated justly. We furiously engage in one activity after another, and often in many activities simultaneously, in an effort to show the world that we are worthy. We strive to avoid being criticized or attacked for some failure. We have an enormous fear of failure because it would leave us vulnerable to those who would destroy us with criticism and shame.

In our struggle to prove our worth and prevent failures, we feel compelled toward greater accomplishments and ever grander goals. If only we could control situations, we could use our intelligence, our energy, and our hard work to make things turn out as they should.

Shame and the Fear of Violation

As titans, we feel shame, envy, and fear of attack. All are rooted in the feeling that our basic integrity—who we are and what we feel—can and will be violated. We fear what others think of us, and we are convinced that they think we are not good enough. Shame is specifically this feeling of being unworthy and inadequate as human beings.

Robert Bly points out that, when our inner sovereignty is not respected by our parents, our teachers, or our society, we not only develop shame, but also become confused about boundaries. When we live as titans, we live with paranoia. We think our boss is setting us up to fail. We are sure that the driver passing us on the right is defeating us in an imaginary race. Or we sense that our lover is holding back from acknowledging our achievements out of jealousy.

As titans we are haunted by the feeling that our friends, bosses, lovers, and powerful people are competing with us. They attack us, seeking to destroy our sense of worth and to steal what we have. Those who have more than we have are shaming us by example; they are revealing our failings. Those who help us must have ulterior motives such as domination and dependency. Those who do not help us are selfish and untrustworthy. Those who desire our friendship want the riches we have to offer. Those who give us gifts expect more in return. We know that we work hard and diligently, yet the fruits of our labor seem to benefit others more than ourselves.

So we frequently feel that we are being cheated, that others are reaping the rewards of our efforts. We become protective of our accomplishments. Rather than sharing the joy of our victories, we erect protective walls to secure our gains. This realm is characterized by the illusion of scarcity, the conviction that there is not enough to go around. Therefore, we must fight not only for our fair share now but also for control, so that we can get ours in the future.

Envy and Entitlement

In this realm we are preoccupied with our desire for what other people have. Our territory is extended beyond simply what we own to include those things that we deserve. If we are unable to obtain what we want, we experience not only frustration, but the pain of undeserved loss. We justify what we want as entitlement, and feel that we have a rightful claim not only to what we have but to what we think we need.

This sense of righteous entitlement shapes our attitude toward others: those who support our activities are friends, and all others are enemies. For the titan, even friends and allies are regarded with suspicion because they might shift positions, becoming enemies. This means that we are continually gauging relative positions, not only with foes, but also with friends. We cannot afford to let our friends become too good, too famous, too successful. Instead of rejoicing in their triumphs we feel alienated from them. We feel envy and shame at not having accomplished all that they have accomplished.

This frame of suspicion and threat means that we mistrust information from other people and cut ourselves off from learning from them. We think that only we can judge what is useful and true. We are preoccupied with the way information is manipulated for competitive ends. We think that one of the few things that we can control is the information that we give other people, and we not only use this to advance our own position but assume that others are doing the same. In fact, we believe that everyone is the same, with the same desires and motives and combative spirit. To us people act out of self-interest and are motivated by the desire for accomplishment, acquisition, status, and power. We distrust protestations to the contrary and demonstrations of alternative motives.

Torn by Desire and Distrust

We are torn between our desire for approval and our distrust of others and their motives. We seek peaceful relationships and a secure sense of belonging, but feel constant distrust and competition. We want to relax and are often exhausted by our constant struggles; yet we fear the consequences of lowering our guard.

We long to fit into the world, but we are convinced that we have to fight for our place and defend it. This means perpetual alienation from other people. We often decide to settle for their respect rather than seeking their love, as this appears safer in the world of competition.

Competing for Esteem

Competition, as such, is neither good nor bad. Competition can support us by giving feedback on our performance, by providing examples of what is possible, by engendering appreciation for the abilities of others, and by creating side-by-side intimacy through fellowship with our competitors. If, however, it is viewed simply in terms of winning and losing and of proving self-worth, it cuts us off from our aliveness. Our competitive urge drives us to be better, smarter and richer than other people. Even religious leaders and spiritual seekers work to become greater, more devout, more skilled and even more humble than anyone else. Yet, when we are concerned with surpassing others, we cut ourselves off from our own best qualities and energies.

This type of competition distances us from other people, making it easy to ignore the feelings and situations of those around us. The desire to win leads us to concentrate on weaknesses of others so that we will look better. We point out their failings as part of our campaign to appear superior. One paradox of competition is that we want to validate our inherent self-worth beyond all comparison by using comparisons with others.

The preoccupation with winning distorts our natural inclination for meaningful action. We search for our arena, our field of competitive advantage. Then we specialize, narrowing the ground of competition to increase our chance of winning. We share less and less with others and lose interest in things outside our sphere of endeavor. Win/lose competitiveness not only alienates us from others but also from our own openness.

To make a virtue of our struggle, we elevate winning to an ideal, excellence to the greatest expression of human nature, and competitiveness to an innate human quality. These qualities, in fact, are learned at home, at school, and at work. The pressure to succeed, however, breeds the fear of failure and shame, which undermines our self-confidence and keeps us trapped in issues of self-esteem.

We use our continual comparisons with others and with our ideals to judge our progress and to map out strategies for the competitive struggle. The success of others is not an indication of our impoverishment, as in the preta realm, but a basis for shame and a target for achievement. We do not want to be less than others, and so we struggle to be superior to them. Comparisons spur us into action. Whereas in the preta realm we internalize the sense of comparison and evaluation, in the realm of the titans we externalize it and try to change our position. We often treat others as obstacles to be moved out of the way, or as data to be manipulated.

We feel shamed by the accomplishments of other people, as though they succeeded in order to spite us. We try to dismiss their sharing as "showing off"—another insult added to the injury of our relative failure.

In our titan frame of mind, we may come to feel that we must be the best at almost any cost. If we cannot exceed everyone else, then we will diminish their successes. If we cannot be taller naturally, we can at least lop off the heads of those around us.

Conceits of Superiority, Inferiority, and Equality

When we inhabit this realm we are prone to three conceits: superiority, inferiority, and equality. The superiority conceit argues, "I am better than you" or "You are worse than me." The inferiority conceit says, "I am worse than you" or "You are better than me." The equality conceits suggests that "I am as good as you," or "You are as bad as me," or "I am as bad as you are."

This last conceit can be the most insidious because it seems virtuous. As titans, we are trying to make everyone at least as bad as we are. If we are angry with our partners and they are calm, we will try to make them upset to show that they are no different and certainly no better than we are. If we confess our failings, we want everyone else to confess theirs to demonstrate that they are no better than us. We want to bring them down to a common level where we can feel equal and can thereby validate ourselves. We enlist the political virtue of equality in the cause of proving that everyone is the same as we are.

Life as a Struggle for Esteem and Power

We see our life history as a contest in which we were wounded by the criticism of others and shamed by our inability to measure up. We feel that we were robbed of our childhood by the assaults of our siblings and parents. We could not enjoy our childhood and had to dream of the time when we would have the power and resources of an adult. Then we would make things right, get what we deserved, and prove our worth to one and all.

In our righteousness we often display our wounds, the badges of honor from our previous battles. As titans, we try to impress people with our valiant battle to overcome a childhood of abuse, or alcoholism, or abandonment. We share stories of how we are overcoming our humble origins and troubled past to win the life that we deserve. When other people share their tales of woe, we feel compelled to let them know how much worse our situation has been.

In this realm we see life as problematic. Unlike the hell realm, where problems are overwhelming, here the problems are calls to battle, challenges to be met, and puzzles to be solved. Our heart posture is that we need to prove something through problem-solving and that we must win the competitive battle of life.

Even our joy in victory and accomplishment is tempered by our fear of future failure and loss, and the possibility of being surpassed by others. We are like old gunfighters who must always face new challengers. At the very moment of possible inner peace, love, and belonging, we are on the lookout for potential threats in this world of endless struggle.

Perfectionism

By refusing to allow for failure or criticism, we become perfectionists. We feel a constant urge to get things right. We fear the consequences of being "wrong" and act defensively when others attempt to give us feedback or to improve on our work. We strive to be the best and to be the masters of all life situations.

Sometimes our efforts seem to pay off. We come close to a goal that, in our minds, will demonstrate our inherent worth. However, if we are "almost" good enough, we get stuck on the "almost," and that obsession can keep us struggling for a long time.

The striving for perfection also reflects dilemmas and inner tensions. We crave superiority but assume that we are inferior. We feel alive only through struggle, but long for peace. We hate our exhaustion, but take pride in never quitting. We fear criticism, but have our own inner critic. Time is always running out, but we must be fully prepared.

Reality of Struggle

While perfection may be our ideal, only our struggle seems real. Even if we do not attain our goals, we affirm our existence and our worth with the thought that we will go down fighting. In fact, the fight becomes even more important than the goals, because we define our aliveness through the sense of struggle. It does not matter that we pursue unattainable dreams, as long as we have made the effort and fought the good fight. We would rather be martyrs in battle for our cause than submit to the possibility of peace and harmony.

In our fascination with the struggle, we substitute the thrill of the moment for the satisfying feelings that come from authentic human sharing and interaction. This thrill of the moment and the energy of battle can even cause us to risk our lives in dangerous actions to achieve these moments and to demonstrate our worth.

Ulcers are symptomatic of this realm, as we constantly try to perform in the face of perpetual insecurity and anxiety. We not only fear the known dangers to our position, but the unknown as well. We want more control, and the more things we try to control, the more risk we run of something going wrong.

The Quest for Personal Power

In our efforts at control and our race to succeed, we become preoccupied with personal power. We work to acquire qualities that will help us compete effectively. We believe that if we are stronger, clearer, more detached, more charismatic, more centered, more articulate, quicker, a better speaker, a better marketer, and more efficient in using time and energy, then we will have the power to control our circumstances. Our excellence will attract support from others and will produce the results we want. In fact, we may even think that our capacity for achievement is limited only by our personal power and that this power is potentially unlimited. This grandiosity inspires us to struggle harder. We are blinded by the fantasy of divine powers. We do not see that we seek excellence and power because we want recognition and control, not because they are a means to achieve our goals.

In the hell realm we are concerned with the power of pain and with our own powerlessness; in the titan realm we know the power of action, and we use it for personal validation. We want to act and be effective, not realizing that the struggle and need to prove something dictates the objectives, thus limiting our behavior to reacting. The real power of our aliveness is thereby distorted and hidden.

Separated from our aliveness, we solve problems but dont resolve them. When we encounter problems, our impulse is to act immediately. We apply pressure to change other people and manipulate our external circumstances rather than reflect inwardly on our own shortcomings. We protect ourselves from a sense of failure by closing off our inner vision. We erect defensive walls that shut us off from those who could help us grow. By refusing to face inner truths, we fail to address our own real weaknesses, and the problematic situations arise again and again.

We get discouraged when we see that we are repeating our old habits, that we are always facing the same barriers to achieving our ultimate victory. We pursue the dream of personal power, hoping to realize our "unlimited potential." Our despair comes from the sense of failure and limitation, and our hope is fed by the lure of unlimited power. Despair can lead to withdrawal into the animal realm of paranoid territoriality, and hope, if even partially realized, can move us into the god realm of self-infatuation.

Avoiding Responsibility

In our titan defensiveness we distort responsibility. Instead of acknowledging our own actions and dealing with the consequences, we become concerned with liability. Rather than responding to consequences according to our ability, we distribute blame and argue about who should pay for damages. We close our eyes to our real role in our own circumstances. We blame the weaknesses of others for our problems and our limited accomplishments. This blame frame also makes us feel more powerful than and superior to those we blame. Even when we offer to help others, we are validating our superior position, hoping to get them to work more ably in our service.

When others object or try to give us feedback on our behaviors and attitudes, we resist them and feel resentful. We resist opportunities to change because we would have to admit our failings and thereby become vulnerable. We resent the feedback because we feel that no one can truly understand us or evaluate us fairly. The shame and resentment subtly feed our anger toward others and propel us into further struggle. We even lose sight of our dreams as we obsess about our resentments and long for the power to make others respect us.

Appealing to the Public

In our drive for respect and approval, we may be seduced by superficial judgments. People will encourage us to show only our most appealing behaviors and to say what they want to hear. We pander to an audience and take public attention as validation, even though it is dependent on outward appearances and manipulated impressions.

This habit of superficiality minimizes the threat to our constructed identity and therefore feels comfortable. We befriend people who are engaged in the same game because there is an implicit agreement that "I won't call you on your game, if you won't reveal mine." With most people we attempt to manipulate their feelings, saying what will maintain their esteem for us and prevent their honest feedback. This further obscures both our feelings and our capacity for insight into our own habits.

When we equate manipulation with success, genuine honesty appears naive and unproductive. Our lives seem to be functioning in high gear, our work resulting in material rewards and fame. Yet underneath this superficial progress, we sense that our integrity has been violated, thus aggravating our insecurity and agitation.

Our dissatisfaction and striving prevent us from finding any natural balance in the world and experiencing harmony within ourselves. Our heart posture of struggle also prevents us from greeting new situations freshly. We become jaded in relating to ourselves and other people. Everything appears to be the same old thing, as we cloak our innate freshness with habitual perceptions and unconscious assumptions.

Spiritual Masquerade of the Warrior

As titans we may enter the spiritual path to improve our personal power and to enhance our self-image and public image. We become warriors in our struggle for perfection. We want to mobilize the energy body in our pursuit of success and excellence. We are preoccupied with the psychic powers and impeccability of the warrior, and view other spiritual aspirants—and even our own teachers—as competitors. We also sense the power of harmony, spontaneity, and authenticity and want these for ourselves to serve our titan goals. However, even though our motivation may begin with desire for personal power, if we continue to practice and grow, the fruits of practice will undermine our quest for power.

Noticing Movement and Harmony

As we reflect on the nature of life, we realize that everything is in perpetual motion. Our bodies are composed of constantly moving atoms, molecules, fluids and energies. Our minds are always in motion and so are our feelings and sensations. We are always moving internally and externally. Breathing, for example, represents the movement of elements into and out of our bodies.

Motion is the expression of Essence in the form of aliveness. All motion is a dance of the elements of existence, which have the potential for an infinite variety of formations. Each moment presents a different configuration of elements and forces; motion is the constant reconfiguration of universal forces. There is always balance and harmony because, from the viewpoint of the whole, there is no fixed point or state from which to judge discord or imbalance.

When astronauts look at the earth from the vantage point of outer space, they are always struck with its beauty. Clouds are part of the texture and movement in the tranquil scene. The storms below the clouds are seen moving over the surface of the earth. Only when we feel uncomfortable on the ground in a storm and treat the clouds as an enemy do we feel conflict. The activities of clouds change from being simply natural phenomena to becoming causes for reaction on our part.

If we are attached to a particular way things should be, such as wanting to perpetuate the beauty of a blossoming rose, then we become distressed when the petals wilt and the plant loses its leaves with the approaching winter. When we realize that this is part of a larger cycle of life in which there is a time for growing, a time for blooming, and a time for dying, we experience the life force at work in every season.

Conflict comes from becoming fixated on one position or feeling, which we then fight to establish and preserve. Then we judge any variations from that desired state to be discordant. If we open our view to include all that is, then the balance becomes more evident and the process of change becomes encouraging rather than threatening. We realize that the Essence is expressed through us, both individually and collectively. Our actions are the form that the divine takes in the moment through our particular personality and behaviors.

Each of us occupies a position in time and space. Even if our consciousness is all-embracing and inclusive, we still have the characteristics of that position, still operate through a personality, and still retain our particular consciousness as the center for experience, but without the assumption of a separate individual self. When we understand our own nature, freed from the quest for a permanent identity, we see ourselves as an expression of universal dynamics and principles.

Lama Govinda beautifully elucidated the nature of harmony as it applies here:

> Harmony, as we know it from music, is the best example of an experience in which law and freedom are fused, and in which these expressions lose their contradictory meaning. A musician does not feel any compulsion in following the laws of musical harmony. On the contrary, the more perfect he is able to express them in his play or his compositions, the more he feels the joy of creative freedom. He is no more a slave to law,

but its master, because he has understood and realized it so profoundly, as to become one with it and to make it the most perfect expression of his own being. Through knowledge we master the law, and by mastering it, it ceases to be necessity, but becomes an instrument of real self-expression and spiritual freedom. The Enlightened One becomes master of the law, the master-artist, in whom the rigid necessity of law is transformed and dissolved into the supreme freedom of harmony.

Fearlessness

Fearlessness comes from understanding that nothing can happen to us that is not consistent with our basic nature, and that aliveness involves living, changing, growing, and dying. Fearlessness is essential for spontaneous action. It allows involvement in all of life without reservation or hesitation. Avoiding evil, ignoring suffering, and withdrawing from life are the path of stagnation. The work here is to be engaged with all human beings and with all the circumstances that they create. When we are fearless we are not shut off from life, but rather openly invite all of the infinite variations of action and feeling that human beings can generate into our awareness.

Skillful Means

On the path of spiritual growth, it is important to honor the skills we have developed even if they resulted from compulsive behavior. Our skills are still skills, and when they are no longer used in the service of compulsions and archaic agendas, they become liberating. We can use the materials of our own development to continue to grow. The ground that we fall on is the same ground we use to push against in getting up. The only thing that delays us is complaining about the ground while we are laying there.

When we operate from the assumption that there is nothing fundamentally wrong with us, that our basic nature is good, and that life is not problematic, we begin to realize that our basic nature is similar to our body's immune system. The body naturally tries to maintain wholeness and health. Even when we abuse it, the body, responding to the essential forces that tend toward integrity, keeps reasserting health. Our soul naturally reasserts significance and constantly manifests meaningful action. What we really want is to develop skillful means in the expression of our aliveness in the world.

Our response to a natural disaster might give us a glimpse of the skillful means we want to embody. We intuitively act to save life in creative ways when a flood threatens our family and community. Our energies are quickly mobilized; we are clear in our objectives; and we act with urgency but without panic. We celebrate our successes with gratitude and unselfconscious joy.

Skillful means involves the full participation of our energies, the spontaneous expression of our creativity, the open sharing of our natural enthusiasm, and the exercise of our talents and abilities in meaningful actions. These actions contribute to the health, well-being, and aliveness of others and to life itself. Skillful means is productive activity combined with the capacity for discernment and what is called "all-accomplishing wisdom."

All-Accomplishing Wisdom

All-accomplishing wisdom combines the emotional warmth of the inner sun of equanimity with the vast space of openness to guide us toward spiritual maturity. Equanimity develops from the perception of the inherently identical nature and interrelatedness of all phenomena and beings. With equanimity we act from the harmony which results from that perception. When we are open, we move beyond self-preoccupation to the willingness to act for the benefit of others, to promote aliveness, and to demonstrate all-embracing love.

Realizing the principle of perpetual movement, our actions are the air we breathe into our aliveness. It is in our nature to act, to do things, to achieve results. While this impulse to act is compulsive when dictated by agendas of validation, it can be liberating when informed by openness, by the desire to create value that frees others, and by the wisdom of Essence.

The seeds of our liberation are rooted in the decomposition of our habit patterns. They sprout and break through the confines of our past selves when our practice creates the appropriate conditions. Spiritual practice loosens the ground, supplies nourishing energy, and shines conscious awareness to fuel our growth. When our flower opens to the radiance of life, our natural potential blossoms as wisdom. This wisdom bears the fruit of our liberation in each fresh moment as we enact the dance of life.

We know this freshness in a baby's quick smile: we immediately become more present and alive. Brilliant colors on a crisp fall morning or a glimpse of a falling star can evoke an impulse of freshness before we can even name what we are responding to. When we spontaneously play, like a kitten with a ball of yarn or a toddler chasing a puppy, we live in the moment, delighted with the freshness of the unknown flow of events. Spiritual work aims to free us from habitual neediness, self-promoting goals, and everyday time and space. Beyond all this, a wisdom arises that meets the world with ever-fresh joy and energy, moment to moment.

This impulse for realization allows other wisdom qualities to come to life, and encourages us in our chosen path. Through conscious (not self-conscious) action, we are transformed again and again until we actually become what we aspire to. The power of our will, no longer tied to habitual patterns of wanting, fearing, and hiding, finds spontaneous, authentic expressions of our relationship to everyone else. The natural harmony of our being and the freshness of our becoming are expressed in our behaviors as our inner realization takes outer form. We naturally and effortlessly harmonize our movements with others in a shared dance. Action balances and unites the inner and outer worlds, the visible and the invisible, and expresses the qualities of the soul through the form of the body.

In following this path, we develop authentic communication, responsibility, humility, and the ability to work with others. When we express our love, our caring, and our dedication, we allow the bonds of friendship to grow and blossom, focusing on improving all lives.

True Responsibility

"True responsibility," Tarthang Tulku states in his book *Skillful Means*, "is an active caring and responsiveness to everything around us, a readiness to do whatever needs to be done. This means that we take responsibility not only for certain obligations, but for every aspect of life, responding to each experience with a dynamic willingness, an openness to life that springs from a deep caring." He points out that true humility involves experiencing ourselves as similar to all human beings, seeing that we share the same ultimate nature, and knowing that we all have strengths and weaknesses. We are all striving to grow.

Working well with others is critical to accomplishing many projects and maintaining community. It also awakens an appreciation for each person's unique contribution, and synergetically gives rise to vital forces and creative energies that are only tapped through cooperating in a task. In developing these qualities, we approach the unknown with freshness and warriorship.

Spiritual Warriorship

Spiritual warriorship is embodied by living each day as if it is our last. Death becomes our ally and guide. Knowing that growing and dying are going on constantly within our bodies, we approach every activity in terms of whether we are willing to die doing it. If it is not worth our life, we move on. As warriors we invest ourselves totally because that is what returns life to us.

Living powerfully in an authentic way expresses aliveness with skillful means. In order to acquire the power of authenticity we must be self-aware, not self-conscious. When we are self-aware we know our basic nature and are not seduced by the trappings of fame and fortune. We relate unpretentiously and gratefully with all people, animals and the environment. We act spontaneously, fearlessly, and congruently with our true nature.

Aspiration Inquiry

This meditation is designed to elicit the true aspiration behind our day-to-day feelings and emotions—what we really want for ourselves and other people. This is an aspiration inquiry into what lies beneath the surface of our reactions, feelings, and beliefs.

Begin the meditation by placing your attention on your palm or your breath, letting your body and mind ease into the process until you feel relaxed and alert. Expand your inner smile throughout your body and be in touch with your purpose and desire to become free through your meditation. Think about an uncomfortable situation you are confronting in your life. Now, methodically inquire into your deeper thoughts, feelings, and intentions concerning this situation.

1. What is the situation I am confronting?
2. What are my beliefs about myself and this situation?

3. What are my feelings and attitudes about this situation?

4. What do I want to do? (Not necessarily what you can or actually would do.

5. For what purpose do I want to do that?

6. Then, what will having that (previous goal) do for me? Continue inquiring with variations of the same questions.

   Some variations are:

   a. What will accomplishing that do for me?

   b. If I have that, what will it mean?

   c. Once I have that, what will that do for me?

7. Continue inquiring until you reach a fundamental intent that involves values such as belonging, harmony, peace, happiness for all, and freedom.

8. Who wants that (belonging, peace, freedom)?

Balance and Seasons of the Emotions

In the second meditation we use the forces and energies of our emotions to balance and grow. When we try to stand up and resist a high surf, we are continually toppled and beaten down. When we ride the surf, we realize that the wave is not the water but the force that moves through the water and through us, and we can relax and float on the waves. We can use the energies and forces of our emotions in a similar way.

After setting up your meditation, locate an energy center at the level of the navel in the middle of your body with the core channel going through it. In this center imagine a caldron or cooking and mixing pot, which will blend your elemental forces so that what is extraneous falls away while the essence of these forces is extracted and distilled.

You want to regard the entire situation of emotions as "not being personal" and as the play of forces. The "not-personalness" of it is also a type of emptiness. It is empty of personal meaning and can be seen as the natural flow of energies.

Compassion arises as a jewel in the caldron in which all things can be transformed and harmonized. This jewel is an expression of Essence or the One. This center becomes a transformation station for both your physical energies and your soul energies.

Now, as you work with an emotion, begin by experiencing the livingness of it. Let any stories connected to the emotion drop off as you go deep into your sensations and then sense the actual movement of energy in the emotion. Examine the nature of the energy involved. Ask, "What is its direction?" Feel its texture—is it wet or dry? Is it soft or brittle? Is it expansive or contractive? Then notice what is missing and consider what is required to establish balance and completeness.

For example, you can recall the emotion of fear and re-experience it in your body. Notice that there are certain muscles that tense, some areas that get cooler while others get hotter. The story associated with the emotional experience may come to mind—notice that it is made up of concepts. Then let the story go, or allow it to run in the background, out of consciousness. Notice the direction of the energy.

Taking that energy from wherever you feel it, draw it into the transformation station of the jewel of compassion. Consider what is left out, what is missing. If the fear is cool and contracted, seek to balance this energy with the complementary energies of warmth and expansiveness. You may feel an inner warmth radiating from the jewel throughout your body, like sunbathing from the inside outward.

Having the sense that you can draw in, mix and blend all of the complementary energies, take everything that the emotion includes and all that had been excluded and reunite them in the jewel of the One. As you do this, more and more of your body will come alive and become part of the dance of the energies. As all of the energies continue to blend, a more harmonious and balanced energy will emerge from the jewel, spreading to all parts of your body and pervading your sense of being.

When you feel stable in this fuller, more balanced energy, then you can examine the story associated with the emotion. Contemplate what you would be like if you were not pushed around by fear. How would you develop, if you were not caught in habitual reactions? Then consider that your fear is an indication that life is presenting you with a demand that you enter into a larger state of being, presenting an opportunity for you to grow. Feel how you would be in this new state of being: larger, fresher, more expansive and harmonious than you have been. As you extract the essential wisdom qualities from fear, feel the cool, reflective aspect of your internal state. Notice that it has a very alert quality within a kind of pause or stillness. The elemental force is alert stillness that, when resisted, is experienced as fear. You may notice that the energy behind fear creates a pause, a space for reflection, listening, and integration.

Taking the emotion of anger as another example, follow the same process of experiencing the aliveness of the feeling. Notice the sensations and their direction and qualities. Determine what is missing. Then blend them all in the jewel of the transformation station. Feel the presence of movement. Sense the way the blended energy radiates from you and the ways in which it gives rise to clarity, to honesty, and to action—the essential qualities behind the energy that you experienced as anger when you operated out of your story. Whereas the energy of fear engenders a stillness and space, the energy of anger gives rise to "showing up" and action.

You can elicit and balance the Essence qualities of each of the primary emotions. This is done in a sequence that reflects the seasons of experience, of action in the world, and of life. Each season develops from the previous one and creates the conditions for that which follows. The cycle of seasons is the turning wheel of change as forces arise out of stillness, grow, blossom, wither, and return to stillness. The ability to dance with the seasons harmonizes actions not only in the context of a particular situation but also in the flow of time.

When a season, as manifest in its corresponding energetic quality, is resisted, the result is the contracted energy of a limiting emotion. We have just worked with the season of winter, with the quality of alert stillness which, when resisted, we know as fear. Then comes the season of spring, with the quality of showing up and making our presence known in the world, which is contracted through our expression of anger.

The season of early summer is characterized by the energy of growth, in which we cultivate the energy of creativity and the quality of fullness of attention. When we contract against the intensity of this process, we experience overwhelming panic, a sense of urgency and rush, and the desire for a solution or relief from inner tension. We get caught up in this desire, reducing everything to mere data in our search for satisfaction of our sense of need. We can work with this urgent desiring in the same way we did with fear and anger to uncover the basic energy of that emotion.

Late summer is a time of richness, blossoming, reaching out, connecting, and relating. It is naturally a time when inner growth gives way to expanding outward to include our environment. A flower sends out a fragrance, not for itself, but to let its surroundings know it is there and to establish a relationship with that which is beyond its immediate boundaries. When this energy of relating and inclusion is contracted against, the environment does not disappear but becomes a source of worry, anxiety, and distraction.

Fall is the season of surrender, of letting go, and of rendering up all the fruits of the stages of growth that led up to it. It is the season when energy withdraws into its source in order to be recycled at another time. When we resist letting go and contract by trying to hang on to the richness that is passing away, we experience loss and the emotion of grief.

Our internal season determines the intensity of our unconscious emotional reactions. A cap left off the toothpaste tube may not bother us in the richness of our internal late summer, but the same small event may trigger a violent explosion when we resist the inner season of spring with outdated habits.

Each emotional contraction is an opportunity to reveal the essential energy that is being resisted. Each offers the possibility of greater aliveness. As we work with the emotions in this way and coalesce the energy in the jewel of compassion at the transformation center, the core channel opens and expands. We may experience heat rising toward the top of our head. The energy that accumulates there may also drip down toward the caldron. As the energies mix, blend, expand, and radiate, we experience aliveness in action.

The true refinement of these practices takes place in our interactions with other people. Our capacity for harmonious action is developed ultimately in our relationships as we work, play, and are intimate. Compassion cannot remain an abstract feeling. Compassion is realized only through action with others.

In modern society, where our survival depends upon communication and interaction much more than upon our hunting, herding, and agrarian skills, we have many opportunities for practicing compassion. The survival and well-being of the entire planet depends on our transcending the quest for power and developing compassionate action and a welcoming environment in which everyone belongs and knows he is significant.

8

Prisoners of Comfort

The Realm of Gods Cut Off from Wonder

As if you could kill time without injuring eternity.
Henry David Thoreau, Walden

The most beautiful thing we can experience is the
mysterious. It is the source of all true art and science.
He to whom this emotion is a stranger, who can no
longer pause to wonder and stand rapt in awe, is as
good as dead; his eyes are closed.
Albert Einstein, What I Believe

A person who believes, as she did, that things fit:
that there is a whole of which one is a part, and that
in being a part one is whole: such a person has no
desire whatever, at any time, to play God. Only those
who have denied their being yearn to play at it.
Ursula LeGuin, The Lathe of Heaven

If one does not understand the way in which the
  enemy—afflictions—exists,
Then in spite of one's lifelong pride of being a
  spiritual person, one will be like a cave.
If one makes no effort in the means of controlling the
  self-grasping within one's own mind,

127

Then although one proclaims vast and profound
spiritual truths, they will be like echoes.

Geshe Rabten

The inhabitants of the god realm are beings who think of themselves as born from lotuses, totally unsullied and pure, and are preoccupied with comfort and enjoyment. Their territory is climate controlled, and mirrors and self-portraits are primary decorations so they can see their own appearance. Each one thinks that he or she has created the world, or that it was created for his or her benefit and entertainment. Everything revolves around the vanities of "self."

Avalokita appears in this realm in the Spiritual Father manifestation with a lute as Vairocana, a sun-like bodhisattva who is brilliant white, representing the qualities of supreme wisdom. He plays beautiful and engaging tunes. Some of the gods are lulled by the music, some begin to swing with the rhythms and tap their feet to the beat, and others sit entranced. Then he suddenly, in mid-verse, stops playing, interrupts the flow, and leaves the gods in a listening space with nothing to listen to. He repeats the process with another melody until he begins to invoke their capacity of listening and to evoke the quality of wonder and surprise.

The Divine Mother, Akashadhatisvari, the "womb of infinite space," invites the gods to find this vast space and wonder within themselves. Each time Vairocana interrupts the music, she says "Oh! What's that?" The gods respond, "Well, there was this beautiful lute music." "No!" she replies suggestively, "I mean after the lute, what was that?" Where Vairocana acts upon the listening of the gods, Akashadhatisvari gets them to listen to their listening. In this way, the gods also become aware of impermanence and change and achieve a sense of the beyond.

IN OUR EFFORTS to secure our own happiness and continuity in the face of change, we may have successes that seem to give us material or spiritual rewards. We experience comfort in material possessions, in status, in power, in achieving more blissful states of mind, in being loved by others, and in our high regard for ourselves. We lose track of hope and fear through sensual pleasures, mental constructs of heavenly inner kingdoms, and preoccupation with "good" feelings. Pain is denied, ignored, or rejected as being irrelevant to achieving bliss, intrusive to our self-esteem, and a sign of unhealthy attitudes and life-style. We actually entertain the notion of endless pleasure and eternal happiness for our bodies and our minds.

Self-Infatuation

This is the realm of the "gods." As gods, our vanities—our images of who we think we are—are concerned with pleasure, beauty, power, wealth, fame, virtue, and pride. Far from being obsessed with our failings and inadequacies, we are fascinated with our own powers and attributes. We admire ourselves, and we are seduced by the comfort and joy that results from this admiration. Conflict, struggle, pain, ugliness, criticism, dissatisfaction, and anger are considered to be dysfunctional to creating the right environment with "good" vibrations. We want to surround ourselves with only those people and things that support our well-being, our self-esteem, our enjoyment, and our happiness. We exorcise negative forces and influences from our lives. For us, the struggle is just about over. We are close to being able to achieve and manifest our unlimited potential through our unlimited personal power.

Preoccupied with Feeling Good

We are concerned with acquiring things not to prove anything, but to experience the joy of what they bring. We are preoccupied with the feelings that are produced as we fixate on our emotional states of well-being. Good feelings must be right and virtuous. Feeling happy, physically good, emotionally expansive, and loving, could not possibly be bad. If others suffer, it is because they have not done enough of the right work to create a supportive inner and outer situation. By cultivating these conditions in our lives, we will reshape the universe into our beatific image.

However, instead of actively working to make the world better, we settle for playing with the image. In fact, we do not create anything. We simply avoid facing ourselves, our problems, our boredom, and the rest of the world. We seek out entertainment, something to occupy our attention in an enjoyable way. We want life to be "fun," as if "fun" is what makes living worthwhile.

In this realm we are addicted to "good feelings and feeling good"—good feelings about ourselves, about our possessions, about the people we know, and about the workings of the universe that brought us personal power, pleasure, and admiration. Our theme song is "Let the Good Times Roll."

Creating Our World of Pleasure

We think that we have finally found the answer to the problem of existence, and it is us. All that is needed is personal magnetism, which will attract what we want into our lives. This magnetism will bring the right partner, wealth, not to mention convenient parking spaces. When we have some degree of success, we think that it resulted from our personal power. This can be very intoxicating. We do not acknowledge other forces in the universe, but concentrate on how we made something happen, not so much by our hard work as by the magnetism of our being.

We avoid effort, seeking the most effortless way to maximize our pleasure and well-being. Unlike the effortless activity that flows from us when we are attuned to our essential nature, in the frame of mind of this realm, the body becomes alienated except to the extent that it provides enjoyment. Strain is an enemy. This alienation pushes us increasingly into our minds, searching for the mental attitudes that produce desirable feelings without the struggle of our body or the need for relationships. We search out ever more rarified practices to gain access to our bliss. We try to live our entire lives in a hypnotic trance.

In fact, we have hypnotized ourselves. We are entranced with ourselves, our beautiful things, our virtuous actions, our admirers, our accomplishments, our thoughts of love, our pleasure, and our power to enjoy. We are entranced with our own existence, as if we were responsible for creating ourselves.

Escaping Life through Comfort

As gods, we retreat into the comforts of our body or our mind or both. The vital functions that culture plays in our growth, in our coping with life transitions, and in our participation in a larger community are distorted by god realm preoccupations. Most of popular culture is designed to seduce us with the pleasures of the body, while classical and higher culture aims to develop the rarified world of the mind. In the context of the god realm, cultural expressions become escapes from the true conditions of life, from death, from others, and from pain. Culture becomes something to consume—and to be consumed by—rather than a vehicle for sharing. Life-style, not authentic expression, becomes the message.

We increasingly become observers and passive participants in life rather than actors. Attached to the media and its techniques of effortlessly occupying our attention, we demand immediate gratification. We feel we have a right to the "good life," like the winner in a lottery commercial. Ideally, we would also remove all causes and forms of suffering from our personal world so that our environment is not contaminated by pain.

Seeking Oneness

In this realm we want to be "one with the universe." We are trying to return to a time when we felt no separation, when the world of our experience seemed to be the only world. We want to recover the experience and comfort of the womb. In the universe of the womb, everything was ours without qualification and was designed to support our existence and growth. Now we want the cosmos to be our womb, as if it were designed specifically for our benefit.

We want satisfaction to flow more easily, naturally and automatically. This seems less likely when we are enmeshed in the everyday affairs of the world. Therefore, we withdraw to the familiar world of what is ours, of what we can control, and of our domain of influence. We may even withdraw to a domain in the mind. Everything seems to come so much easier in the realm of thought, once we have achieved some modest control over our minds. Insulating ourselves from the troubles of others and of life, we get further seduced by the seeming limitlessness of this mental world.

In this process of trance formation, we try to make every sound musical, every image a work of art, and every feeling pleasant. Blocking out all sources of irritation, we retreat to a self-proclaimed "higher" plane of being. We cultivate the "higher qualities of life," not settling for a "mundane" life.

Masquerade of Higher Consciousness

The danger for those of us on a spiritual path is that the practices and the teachings can be enlisted to serve the realm rather than to dissolve our fixations and open us to truth. We discover that we can go beyond sensual pleasure and material beauty to refined states of consciousness. We achieve purely mental pleasures of increasing subtlety and learn how to maintain them for extended periods. We think we can maintain our new vanity and even expand it to include the entire cosmos, thus vanquishing change, old age, and death. Chogyam Trungpa Rinpoche called this process "spiritual materialism."

For example, we use a sense of spaciousness to expand our consciousness by imposing our preconception of limitlessness on the cosmos. We see everything that we have created and "it is good." Our vanity in the god realm elevates our self-image to the level of the divine—we feel capable of comprehending the universe and the nature of reality.

We move beyond our contemplation of limitless space, expanding our consciousness to include the very forces that create vast space. As the creator of vast space, we imagine that we have no boundaries, no limits, and no position. Our mind can now include everything. We find that we do not have concepts for such images and possibilities, so we think that the Divine or Essence must be *not* any particular thing we can conceive of, must be empty of conceptual characteristics.

Thus our vain consciousness, as the Divine, conceives that it has no particular location, is not anything in particular, and is itself beyond imagination. We arrive at the conclusion that even this attempt to comprehend emptiness is itself a concept, and that emptiness is devoid of inherent meaning. We shift our attention to the idea of being *not* not any particular thing. We then come to the glorious position that nothing can be truly stated, that nothing has inherent value. This mental understanding becomes our ultimate vanity. We take pride in it, identify as someone who "knows," and adopt a posture in the world as someone who has journeyed into the ultimate nature of the unknown.

In this way we create more and more chains that bind us and limit our growth as we move ever inward. When we think we are becoming one with the universe, we are only achieving greater oneness with our own self-image. Instead of illuminating our ignorance, we expand its domain. We become ever more disconnected from others, from communication and true sharing, and from compassion. We subtly bind ourselves ever more tightly, even to the point of suffocation, under the guise of freedom in spaciousness.

Spiritual Masquerades of Teacher and Devoted Student

As we acquire some understanding and feel expansive, we may think we are God's special gift to humanity, here to teach the truth. Although we may not acknowledge that we have something to prove, at some level we are trying to prove how supremely unique and important we are. Our spiritual life-style is our expression of that uniqueness and significance.

Spiritual teachers run a great danger of falling into the traps of the god realm. If a teacher has charisma and the ability to channel and radiate intense energy, this power may be misused to engender hope in students and to bind them in a dependent relationship. The true teacher undermines hope, teaches by the example of wisdom and compassion, and encourages students to be autonomous by investigating truth themselves, checking their own experience, and trusting their own results more than faith.

The teacher is not a god but a bridge to the unknown, a guide to the awareness qualities and energy capacities we want for our spiritual growth. The teacher, who is the same as we are, demonstrates what is possible in terms of aliveness and how to use the path of compassion to become free. In a sense, the teacher touches both aspects of our being: our everyday life of habits and feelings on the one hand and our awakened aliveness and wisdom on the other. While respect for and openness to the teacher are important for our growth and freedom, blind devotion fixates us on the person of the teacher. We then become confined by the limitations of the teacher's personality rather than liberated by the teachings.

False Transcendence

Many characteristics of this realm—creative imagination, the tendency to go beyond assumed reality and individual perspectives, and the sense of expansiveness—are close to the underlying dynamic of wonderment. In wonder, we find the wisdom qualities of openness, true bliss, the realization of spaciousness within which all things arise, and alignment with universal principles. The god realm attitude results in superficial experiences that fit our preconceptions of realization but that lack the authenticity of wonder and the grounding in compassion and freedom.

Because the realm itself seems to offer transcendence, this is one of the most difficult realms to transcend. The heart posture of the realm propels us to transcend conflict and problems until we are comfortable. The desire for inner comfort, rather than for an authentic openness to the unknown, governs our quest. But many feelings arise during the true process of realization. At certain stages there is pain and disorientation, and at others a kind of bliss that may make us feel like we are going to burst (if there was something or someone to burst). When we settle for comfort we settle for the counterfeit of realization—the relief and pride we feel when we think we understand something.

Because we think that whatever makes us feel good is correct, we ignore disturbing events, information, and people and anything else that does not fit into our view of the world. We elevate ignorance to a form of bliss by excluding from our attention everything that is non-supportive.

Preoccupied with self, with grandiosity, and with the power and radiance of our own being, we resist the mystery of the unknown. When we are threatened by the unknown, we stifle the natural dynamic of wonder that arises in relation to all that is beyond our self-intoxication. We must either include vast space and the unknown within our sense of ourselves or ignore it because we do not want to feel insignificant and small. Our sense of awe before the forces of grace cannot be acknowledged for fear of invalidating our self-image.

Above the Law

According to our self-serving point of view, we are above the laws of nature and of humankind. We think that, as long as what we do seems reasonable to us, it is appropriate. We are accountable to ourselves and not to other people, the environment, or society. Human history is filled with examples of people in politics, business, and religion who demonstrated this attitude and caused enormous suffering.

Unlike the titans who struggle with death, we, as gods, know that death is not really real. We take comfort in the thought that "death is an illusion." The only people who die are those who are stuck and have not come to the true inner place beyond time, change, and death. We may even believe that we have the potential to develop our bodies and minds to such a degree that we can reverse the aging process and become one of the "immortals."

A man, walking on a beach, reaches down and picks up a pebble. Looking at the small stone in his hand, he feels very powerful and thinks of how with one stroke he has taken control of the stone. "How many years have you been here, and now I place you in my hand." The pebble speaks to him, "Though to you, I am only a grain of sand in your hand, you, to me, are but a passing breeze."

Swinging to Extremes

In this realm, we become extreme. We want to cultivate the extreme of self-confidence, the ultimate in personal power, the farthest reaches of excellence, and the best in the good life. Any virtue carried to its extreme tends to become a vice. We make our particular virtue a fixation rather than a spontaneous response.

Our god realm mentality often emerges when we begin to break out of the other realms. As we experience our inner witness and the initial expansiveness that follows, we think that this spaciousness is true realization. We realize that we *are* bigger than our problems. We *can* feel relief and comfort. We *do* have powers and resources. Like a pendulum we swing from a sense of inadequacy, powerlessness and struggle to one of grandiosity. Not only is the newfound sense of ourselves a relief from our pain, but it seduces us with the feeling that we can create the world of our dreams.

As we free ourselves from fixations and the need to prove ourselves to others, we are susceptible to the intoxication of gods. We think we are no longer answerable to any authority other than our own. While freedom from inner and outer authority is important to our growth, we lose our ability to respond in the self-enclosed perspective of a god. When we deny the reality of our situation and that of other people, we become unresponsive and thereby irresponsible. Then, at the first challenge to our new self-esteem, our old habits of self-doubt reappear. Once again, like a pendulum, we swing back into our pain.

As gods we try to cover up our fears of helplessness and insignificance. Poised on the edge of falling into the hell realm, we protect ourselves with elaborate strategies of denial and distraction. Underneath our apparent bliss is profound terror—of death, of losing power, wealth, fame, and beauty, and of sinking into a melancholy in which everything seems meaningless.

Vanity

The issue is not the ego. Having a personality and the capacity for self-reference is not a problem as such. What blocks our growth is our ego's vanity, the aspect of our self-regard that is attached to particular opinions about who and what we are. Vanity means "futile," "without value," "worthless," "emptiness," and having an "erroneous opinion" of oneself. Vanity is our self-image. We attach truth and great significance to this image. We will even stake our lives on it. However, if we examine it carefully, we find it to be inherently worthless.

Noticing Impermanence

The first step on the path to awakening from our god realm trance is acknowledging impermanence. Entertain the thought that the only permanent thing is change: whatever comes will go; whatever arises will disappear; and whatever is gained will be lost.

Impermanence and the empty vastness into which all things go are what we have been hiding from. Facing these stark truths can be terrifying, but it will allow us to open to their other side—wonder. This wonder knows that creation is continually occurring, that life springs forth unceasingly. So, whatever comes *will* go—and life comes every moment; whatever arises *will* disappear—and new marvels continuously arise; whatever is gained *is* lost—and this creates the space for new blossoming to occur.

We know wonder in the birth of a child. After all the effort, boredom, pain, and worry comes a moment when suddenly a new spirit is present that was not in the world before. Walking to the edge of the Grand Canyon for the first time hints at this wonder, the awe of the world opening more fully than we have ever known. Wonder is the joy of relaxing into the unknown in this very moment.

When we have wonder, we also can acknowledge the presence of other people. Depending upon what we fear about relationships and what we feel compelled to prove to other people about ourselves, we risk falling into one or more of the other realms. Yet if we authentically open our hearts, we feel the wonder of the mysteries of life.

When we intentionally and lucidly surrender ourselves to a state of helplessness and hopelessness, we see the miracle of our own existence and experience the wonder at all that shows up. We then feel gratitude for our lives.

The King Who Dreams of Being Naked

Once there was a king who had everything he could ever want—a beautiful kingdom, delicious food, adoring subjects and laws that maintained proper behavior, dress, and order. He lived in the most wonderful world he could imagine.

One day, while slightly intoxicated from drinking a very precious wine that was given to him as a gift, he fell asleep upon his throne. As he slept, he began to dream. In this dream he found himself naked in a desert. At first he did not know what to do, since others had always taken care of him. He wandered about the desert in one direction, then another, searching for some place of refuge.

Panicked in his dream of being lost, the king tossed and turned in his sleep. His wives and retainers became concerned as they watched his restless sleep.

In the dream, the king spotted the glimmer of a city in the distance and made his way toward it. He stumbled across the hot sand and rock while the relentless sun baked his skin. As he approached the outskirts of his destination, he recognized his own castle. He was heartened by the thought of returning home to the comforts of his chambers and away from the harsh and painful world of the wild. He quickened his pace even though he was exhausted, bruised, and weak from hunger.

Crossing an open field to reach the gates of the city, he remembered that he had proclaimed an edict against nakedness. He had wanted to protect his kingdom from the naked "bums" who came from the wilderness to beg. The edict stated that all people who appeared naked in public were to be immediately killed and buried. He stopped in his tracks, deciding that he had better think this through.

But it was too late. The trumpets sounded the troops to arms; the drawbridge was lowered; and a company of soldiers rode toward the naked intruder. He panicked and started to flee, running as fast as he could. Realizing that the soldiers on horseback were much faster, he jumped into a briar patch to hide. The soldiers knew he was around somewhere and dismounted in their search. The naked man, knowing that he must find a better hiding place, buried himself in the sand. Before long he felt like he was going to suffocate. He coughed and choked.

As the king coughed and sputtered in his sleep, everyone became alarmed. His chief physician shook him and rang a bell in his ear to awaken him. As the king opened his eyes and cleared his head, he heard the trumpets sounding the alarm that someone was naked at the perimeter of the city. The king jumped to his feet and shouted to his guards to stop the soldiers from harming the intruder.

The guards set out immediately with the king close behind to stop the soldiers from carrying out the edict. As they approached the area of the briar bushes, they saw that the soldiers had unearthed a man and were beating him. He kept yelling to them, "I am the king."

The guards stopped the soldiers from inflicting more pain on the helpless wretch. The king, dressed only in his royal robe, caught up to the gathering and instructed them not to kill the naked intruder. The man said, "You shouldn't kill me, that's right, because I am the king." The soldiers were dismayed. They pointed out that they were simply doing their duty by carrying out the edicts of the king.

The king turned to the man, covered him with his robe, and asked, "Since you are the king, will you grant my request to repeal the edict forbidding and punishing nakedness?" The man replied that he would. The king then placed his crown on the man's head, exclaimed "Wonderful!", and danced naked into the desert.

Delight and Wonder

The god realm capacity for enjoyment can also lead to appreciation and delight. The deeper nature of these virtues is obscured by addiction and fear. However, the desire for peak experiences expresses the genuine desire for aliveness. The self-infatuation reveals the wish to be loved and to love. The search for comfort grows out of the longing for connection and belonging.

When we awaken from the self-indulgent stupor of a god, we see the richness that always surrounds us. We shift from traveling in reverse to going forward. The change in perspective and direction is initially disorienting. Gradually, we find the steering so much easier because we are going toward our aliveness. We also realize that we developed skills in the difficult task of driving backwards. Appreciation and delight now can flow naturally in the wonder of all situations, not simply of those that we had found stimulating or entertaining.

As we gaze with awe into the vastness of the night sky or delight in the incessant activity of an ant colony, we peel away the layers of our self-concerns. With uncontrived wonder we open to our own aliveness and the vitality of the world around us. We appreciate the natural principles that create and sustain aliveness. We become committed to the living moment and to the aliveness in all beings.

Being Committed to Growth

Being committed to our aliveness means continuing to work on ourselves in order to grow, to mature, and to expand our capacities. We relax into our aliveness naturally seeking responsibility, activity and growth. We do not settle for a blissful state of being or for spectacular accomplishments because aliveness never stops or becomes static.

We are filled with wonder at everything and everybody. We feel "wonderful." When we are preoccupied with ourselves and with defending a particular identity, we are terrified of vastness, of the inherently empty quality of all phenomena, and of change. When we release our self-image from having to be the universe, we open to the richness that *is* the universe.

Searching for Essence

Conscious work also opens us to the nature of Essence. Essence cannot be defined; it is beyond words, concepts, and descriptions. It is the context or space from which, within which, and to which all contexts and spaces arise. It is empty of any specific qualities and includes them all. It is the fundamental or absolute nature and foundation of all reality.

To discover this we search for the building blocks of reality. We explore the inner nature of experience, phenomena, and things. As we break things down into ever more elementary components, we come to discrete moments in the present that we cannot grasp conceptually, linguistically, or experientially. They are empty, even of the concept of emptiness. As Baker Roshi says, "All you can determine is that they don't exist in the past, they don't exist in the future, and in the present you can't grasp them."

Essence cannot be understood. This does not mean that we and the world do not exist, but simply that the true nature of all phenomena is beyond concepts and habitual experience. It cannot be discovered by ordinary thinking or communicated by language that polarizes things into existence and non-exist-ence, into real and unreal, and into assertion and negation. We cannot understand or seek to have dominion over Essence through these or any set of categories, because nothing exists conceptually.

We must not abandon thinking, for it is essential to functioning, but we need to realize the limitations of concep-tual perception. Then, in our spiritual work, we can direct our effort to the more fundamental non-conceptual type of percep-tion.

In this non-grasping, non-conceptual perceiving, we move beyond the desire to know and we allow reality to be essential-ly indeterminate. With practice, we stop habitually labelling and organizing our life. As we transcend the urge to impose conceptual boundaries and attributions upon phenomena, we include more of "what is." When we are not bound by "this" or "that" or "this and that," we include "this," "that," "every-thing," and "no-thing." Our attention begins to expand into awareness rather than contract around vanity.

Conventional and Profound Reality

When we realize this openness, we understand two aspects of reality and two types of wisdom—conventional and profound. In conventional reality everything is relative. With conventional wisdom, we act "as if" things exist and "as if" we can accumulate knowledge about them, interact with them, affect them, and be affected by them. Profound wisdom invol-ves knowing that things do not inherently exist, that profound or absolute reality is beyond our thinking and all our "as ifs," and that *Essence is.* With profound wisdom, we act with the realization of emptiness and the knowledge of both the con-ventional and profound aspects of the world. Essence is not determined by the relative or the absolute, by the "as if" or by emptiness. It includes both but is not defined by them.

Delighting in the Rhythms of the Unknown

Compassion moves us beyond self into non-self, and wonder opens us to the unknown. This means that we can experience surprise, not in the sense of being startled but of being delighted. We rejoice at the delight of wonder and radiate that rejoicing to others. Our rejoicing presence can be felt as gentle sunlight and heard as the vibrant music of the spheres.

When we tune into the rhythms of the universe, we open to the cycles of life and death and to the inner seasons of our own growth. We relax into the flow of life and participate in the wonder of it all. We plant the seeds of our intentions, nourish their growth through our attention and activities, share their rewards as they blossom and bear fruit, and let go as they wither and return to the earth.

We use, rather than resist, both our inner cycles and the outer cycles of nature. Like the snake that sheds its skin as it grows and leaves its old appearance behind, we die to our former selves, go through an awkward, vulnerable period, and grow into a new self to continue the process. Completeness is the unqualified participation in life, not the validation of our identity or personal significance.

Surrendering Our Attainments

In spiritual work, when we realize an attainment the first requirement is to surrender it. We don't try to own it. This would simply freeze it as an object of pride and a burden to be lived up to. Instead, we acknowledge this gift of grace and offer it up to the service of other people. The word "surrender" means "through rendering," or to offer oneself to someone or something beyond ourselves.

Inquiring About Our True Nature

The first meditation is an inquiry into our true nature. Begin by placing your attention and recalling your intention to become free in this very meditation for yourself and the benefit of all people. Then imagine going back to a time before you were born. Imagine the way you naturally were before your existence, before the events and decisions in your life. Notice how this feels. Notice your natural radiance. Notice how this true nature affects your body sensations now, your breathing, your posture and your energy. Inquire, "Who knows these feelings?" Continue inquiring. Then abide, relaxing all effort and allowing everything to arise in the space of simply abiding as presence.

Divine Abidings

The second meditation is called the Divine Abidings. In this process, after placing your attention and recalling your purpose, visualize or sense that all beings are in the space around you and contemplate their suffering. Think of the suffering of your parents and of those close to you. Open your heart to their physical and emotional difficulties and realize that, like you, they wish to be free of all suffering. Repeat this process with acquaintances and with people you may not like or get along with, realizing that they, too, are governed by the same habitual patterns that govern you. Open your heart to them. Extend this to all beings.

Begin the next stage of this meditation by accessing a series of divine-like qualities within yourself. When you feel your body and mind pervaded by a particular divine quality, radiate it out, filling all space with the radiance of that quality. The following qualities make up the divine abidings or states of being:

1. HONORING - a friendliness with respect, a sense of awe and wonder at the fact of being.

2. LOVING-KINDNESS - the active alleviation of the suffering of others with unqualified love.
3. REJOICING - the act of manifesting and expressing joy, the celebration of life and aliveness.
4. EQUANIMITY - the harmonious, open, balanced, undisturbed center of spaciousness, a detached serenity and calm clarity that values all.

Access each quality by recalling a time when you were the recipient of that quality and also a time when you gave it to others. For example, recall a time when you were honored as well as a time when you were feeling honor for someone else. Let this quality of honoring spread throughout your body and radiate from every cell. Radiate it to your parents and loved ones. Then to your friends and acquaintances. Radiate this quality to all people and beings. Then repeat this process for each of the remaining divine qualities: loving-kindness, rejoicing, and equanimity.

From Prison to Freedom

When we are trapped in the god realm, we need to examine not only ourselves and our habits, but also the world around us. The work that leads to awakening includes listening to a sound and asking "Where does sound come from?" and "Where does it go?" As we begin to awaken, we view the vastness of the universe and investigate the nature of space. We explore how everything and everybody is related, and how we all contribute to making a shared world. We tap our own creative energies and open to the creativity of other people, which is being expressed continually, moment to moment. And we learn how to expose ourselves to all aspects of human experience and to rejoice in the variety and splendor of the universe. We appreciate the principles that govern all phenomena and express our aliveness in everything we do. We realize the inherent emptiness of all phenomena, all activities, all concepts, all feelings, and all accomplishments, and we rejoice in the freedom of that realization.

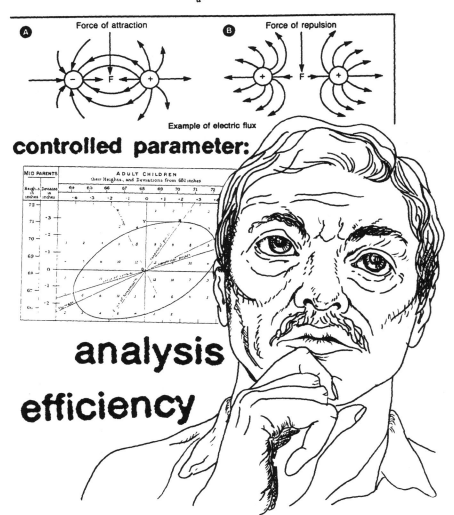

Coulomb's Law

Force of attraction of repulsion,

$$F = \frac{8.99 \times 10^9 \times Q_1 \times Q_2}{d^2} \text{ newtons}$$

Force of attraction

Force of repulsion

Example of electric flux

controlled parameter:

analysis

efficiency

9

Living Without Doubt
Human Realm Concepts
vs Direct Experience

The trouble about arguments is, they ain't nothing
but theories after all, and theories don't prove nothing, they only give you a place to rest on a spell
when you are tuckered out butting around and
around trying to find out something there aint no
way *to* find out.

Mark Twain

Our mind is capable of passing beyond the dividing
line we have drawn for it. Beyond the pairs of op-
posites of which the world consists, new insights
begin.

Herman Hesse

The aim of an artist is not to solve a problem ir-
refutably, but to make people love life in all its count-
less, inexhaustible manifestations.

Leo Tolstoy

*In the human realm, the human beings try to possess everything,
even their own experience and their future. They are continually*

149

naming things, developing concepts about phenomena, and placing meaning in themselves, other people, and things. They want to grasp and own their lives in order to have value. They hunger for value from people, places, things and knowledge. They feel that they have attained a measure of control and may even find happiness when they understand things fully enough. Their sense of presence is held hostage by their explanations and their attempts to make everything fit into their conceptual schema. They transform people and situations into data. They have big heads, large hands that try to manipulate things, and little necks.

Avalokita appears to human beings as the Spiritual Father Ratnasambhava—source of value. He is radiant yellow, rides a horse, and projects the radiance of "presence." Sometimes he shows up in a yellow robe as a monk who has nothing, having renounced people, places and things. He wanders from one place to another without attachments and possessions. Yet he has a value that glows from him. It is his presence.

Mamaki, the Divine Mother manifestation, is the mother of everything. She treasures each thing for being itself. She loves everyone and everything just the way they are. Without having to do anything, without having to own anything, without having to be anything, each is loved by virtue of who he or she is. She invites human beings to experience a sense of unconditional value for their own existence, their own presence, and the fact of being themselves.

They both demonstrate equanimity. They relate to everything as having value, conveying a sense of the essential equality of all beings and of all things. In addition, he generates value from nothing, representing the richness of presence in the space of nothing. She shows how to appreciate the value of each thing in its very presence without it having to be, have, or do anything else.

AS HUMAN BEINGS, our minds can use feelings, images, metaphors, and words to create an infinite variety of inner worlds. These thought forms determine our perceptions, guide our decisions, and direct our actions. Thoughts appear to have a life of their own in which they have real meanings, relate to other thoughts, produce results, and can overcome all the forces of nature. In our efforts to be masters of the world, we rely upon this unique human capacity for conceptual thinking. We enlist the power of imagination in the service of our quests, which themselves are defined and enlarged by the same imagination.

Giving the Mind Dominion Over Life

To give coherence and structure to our efforts, we construct a palace of images, concepts, metaphors, stories, and plans. In the human realm, we enthrone our mental capacities and give them dominion over every aspect of our lives.

We think best when we know where we stand. We want to know "Who am I?", "What is real?", and "Why am I here?" We become obsessed with proving our own reality and worth in the face of doubt, the unknown, the unpredictability of change, and the vastness of the universe. Compelled by these concerns, we enter the twilight zone of the human realm. We want to own our experience so that we know we are the person who has had the experience. We cling to the territory of our experience.

Owning Experience

In this quest to own experience, we try to capture everything in concepts through our understanding. We are like hunters seeking the prey of understanding that, when consumed, will satisfy our hunger for ownership. We want dominion over our experience, our world, and our lives. We think we can tame the forces of nature and the power of existence through thoughts. With intellectual capacities we attempt to reduce the unknown to the understandable and the mysterious to the explicable.

Making Sense

Given our fear of confusion, our sense of well being in this realm comes from understanding. We not only avoid the confusion of complexity but also anything that seems unknown or unknowable. We have a limited tolerance for "not knowing." In fact, our mind will usually attempt to generate answers or solutions within seconds of recognizing a question or problem.

Through understanding the world becomes less intimidating, more malleable, and even familiar. Understanding suffering relieves the tension of confusion and somewhat satisfies the desire for connection. Our sense that we understand—not that in reality we *do* understand—makes us feel more secure and provides an inner self-validation.

When we are preoccupied with understanding, we want everything to be coherent. We construct a coherent system of concepts and a coherent system of expressions for those concepts. They are coherent because they make sense to us. This sense derives from perceiving that something fits—fits things that we already know, fits in terms of being consistent, fits into our experience.

Our early body experience is the primary basis for our sense of fit. As infants and children we initially developed a spatial sense of ourselves. We were here, and something we wanted was there. We took things that were outside of us and put them inside. We knew that something was real when we could put it into our mouth and try to eat it.

We are eating machines that use food for more than growth and survival. We eat to feel good, to satisfy the tension of desire, to sense our own reality, and to make what is outside of us a part of us. Metaphorically, our minds operate in a similar way. We nourish our identities with information and concepts. With information and concepts, we validate our reality, relieve inner tensions through recognition and understanding, feel good through experiences captured as happy memories, and make the entire universe part of our inner world. In this way, we experience the sense of ownership and belonging.

Binding Life

Our passion to devour further energizes our efforts to bind life to our will. We want to tie everything down through our concepts, placing the world under our control and in the service of our agendas. We bind space by making maps of territory; we bind time by writing history and making plans; we bind feelings by making them memories and problems to be solved; we bind relationships by making agreements; we bind thinking by making science; we bind action by making strategies, rules, and laws; we bind communication by making organizations; we bind survival by making economics and politics; and we bind life by making systems of understanding.

In the human realm we think life will be perfect when we can perfectly figure it all out. As soon as everything is perfectly understood, then we will become one with that perfection through our understanding.

Preoccupied with Meaning

We grant more significance to descriptions of our experience than to experience itself. Meaning is important to us. We define the meaning of experiences so that we know their extent, can specify their nature, place them in our world view, and end any doubt about them. The word define means "to bring to an end" and "to fix upon;" in other words, by defining experience we bring confusion and doubt to an end and fix upon a specific concept of its meaning and significance.

We use meaning to build contexts. Our meanings not only build a frame of reference for ourselves but we attempt to build frames of reference for other people through our explanations. The way we think forms our preconceptions, and our preconceptions determine what we see. The purpose is to make life more manageable and to avoid being overwhelmed by events and the chaos of phenomena. We seek understanding as a fortress against the pain of confusion and as a weapon to secure ourselves in the future. We want to be masters of our own fate, able to determine experience and create the future.

As Cassius states in Shakespeare's *Julius Caesar:*

> Men at some time are masters of their fates:
> The fault, dear Brutus, is not in our stars,
> But in ourselves, that we are underlings.

In this intellectual process, we "object-ify" events and processes so we can subject them to our mental manipulations. One of the bibles of this realm is the dictionary. It gives us authoritative information on the meaning of words. To the extent that we think in words, the dictionary assists us in determining the meaning of our own inner world. However, these meanings are explained by other words, which themselves are explained by other words, and so on. The dictionary is a good example of the relational nature of our conceptual world. Each concept is created out of, or in relation to, the one before. It is a self-contained system, like the circular motion of a constantly turning wheel.

Possessing Process and Time

We even use concepts to turn processes and activities into possessions, capturing them through metaphors and words. We nominalize—that is, we make processes and activities into things in our minds. We perform a superficial alchemy by treating a process as a thing, and by using the magic of words and grammar to transform the non-graspable into linguistic objects by changing verbs into nouns. By objectifying processes, we impose properties on them that give us a way of relating to them, of understanding them in terms of our experience, and of evaluating them.

Using the magic of language, we are thus able to hold in our minds that which cannot be possessed. For example, we transform the process of relating into relationship, loving into love, performing into performance, feeling into feelings and emotions, sensing into sensations, and thinking itself into thoughts. We develop concepts such as "struggle," "frustration," "anger," "suffering," "mind," "satisfaction," "enlightenment," and "freedom." As long as we get a vague sense of recognition within ourselves on using, hearing, or reading those words, we think we know what they mean, and that they are real. This also allows us to use the terms possessively in phrases like "having love," "having sex," and "getting a relationship." While this device for making references and concepts may be useful, it can increase our confusion rather than create the conditions for clarity.

We reduce time to an object as a way of managing change and forestalling death. Since "life is a possession," our fear is that "time as a changer" will take our youth and our life from us. By objectifying time and segmenting it into manageable units, we hope to get a measure of control. We make schedules and calendars to fill the future with our events. We expect to be going places and doing things. We make ourselves the constant in the variety of anticipated meetings, as if this will create a semblance of permanence. We feel that if we could plan our future we might hold back the flow of time. Death is not scheduled in our datebook.

When conflicts, pain, and contradictions arise, they do not fit our plans. We become preoccupied by our confusion rather attending to what is really happening. We feel entitled to an explanation when bad things happen to us, but the world does not care what we think, it simply is. Our failure to accept that fact leads to frustration and resentment and we retreat into our world of thoughts and fantasies.

Disassociating from Reality

When we step out of what we think of as us and into a more remote point of view, we disassociate from our immediate experience. By disassociating we look at ourselves as if the person acting and feeling is someone else. This is useful in creating a pause for self-reflection, but as a habit it alienates us from our actions and experiences and fragments our mental and emotional identities.

When we are disassociated, we may act in ways we do not like out of frustration, anger, or resentment. Because we do not feel that "we" are doing them, we become capable of performing acts that, upon reflection, would horrify us. In our own minds, we did not "mean to." We feel as though some other person inside of us took over and acted out the intense feelings, and we did not know how to stop them.

This type of fragmentation frequently occurs in situations of abuse. When we are abused, we may disassociate in order not to feel the pain. We rationalize the abusive behavior as unintentional or influenced by alcohol, drugs, or an overwhelming feeling.

From being abused, we may internalize the abusive behavior patterns, and not feel responsible. Then, as abusers ourselves, we feel removed from our actions, out of control, and possessed by emotions, drugs or alcohol. When we are abused, our disassociation allows some part of us to feel that we did not deserve that treatment, no matter what we were told or believed at the time. When we are abusive, disassociation preserves our sense of worth, because we know that at heart we are better people than that.

We can break these patterns of victimization and abuse only if we examine them. We need to acknowledge the wounding, the alienation, the fragmentation, and the self-deception that are occurring in ourselves and in our relationships.

Personal Mythology

Examining our life situation, we can deepen our exploration by telling our story as our personal mythology. As a tool for reflection and growth, this is an important vehicle for bringing habitual patterns of thinking, feeling and behaving into awareness. Our investigation and learning need to be open for real insight to occur, and the entire process must be free of the search for self-righteous validation.

When we are stuck in the human realm world, we are in danger of enlisting our story-telling in the service of vanity. Then we glorify rather than dissolve our fixated identity. As human realm heroes, we elevate to the level of tragedy our efforts to realize our confused ideals.

If we lack the appropriate way of viewing mythology, we do not realize that the true hero's journey, under the guise of finding a missing treasure, a missing monarch, or a missing love, is really about discovering the missing key to the domain of the authentic life. However, the human realm mentality mistakes the intensity of our desires for authenticity, the process of problem solving for a journey of growth, intention for embodiment, novelty for that which is essential, the relief and comfort of understanding for freedom, and the sense of knowing for the realization of wisdom.

We want to prove our worth and give meaning to our past. We get a handle on our past by describing experiences and events to ourselves in a way that makes sense of our feelings now. We look for meaning and explanation in the feeling tone of our memories and in the reactions of others, instead of relating to our direct experience of the moment.

To make our stories understandable and palatable to ourselves, we delete what we don't like and ignore what seems irrelevant. We distort what doesn't fit our knowledge or desires, and we exaggerate what seems important. These deletions, distortions, and exaggerations occur mostly in our unconscious, and fit everything into existing frameworks of meaning. We will even suppress joy if it does not fit into our understanding.

Our life history is part of our personal science of what is real, and our explanations of reality are sacred to us. We would rather experience physical pain than the mental pain of confusion or being wrong. Validation of our point of view seems more important than the authenticity of our actions, the quality of our relationships, and the nature of our immediate experience. We cannot tolerate incongruence between life and our mental constructs. We criticize other points of view, often dismissing them as irrelevant or ignorant.

Seeking Belonging and Immortality

In our fantasies about ourselves as heroes, we seek entrance to the kingdom of belonging and immortality. We imagine living eternally in a world of validation, comfort, and beauty. Yet when we compare our performance to our ideals, we feel perpetual dissatisfaction. We think that if only we knew and understood more, we could discover the answers to life and death, as if these are riddles to be solved. We want to figure out the meaning of existence, the purpose of our particular life, and the key to immortality.

If only we can find the right formula, then we will achieve our desires. In our human realm hallucination, we are limited only by our constricted imagination, our lack of will, our lack of commitment, and our information. To us it may appear that information is the key to all the rest. With information we can direct our imagination, give purpose and meaning to our will, know what we are committing ourselves to, and know how to use all of these effectively and efficiently.

Since we process information with our thoughts, we reduce everything to thoughts—image thoughts, feeling thoughts, and verbal thoughts. Nothing, no matter how complex or vast, escapes our attempt at comprehension through thought. Our early successes in translating vague activities and feelings into understandable concepts leads us to believe that everything is subject to being understood given enough time, intelligence, and effort. We boil it all down to a concept and a label and by so labeling, we think we can reduce the universe to our level of understanding.

Consistency and Our Use of Science

In the rarified world of abstract thought, we feel that permanence is found in consistency. Those things that can be abstractly and independently validated according to some irrefutable logic become eternal truths. We develop systems of abstract language and explanations that we call sciences, each having its own "logic." Even the spiritual is viewed from this perspective in the form of "theology"—"the science of things divine."

Academic institutions are the palaces in which abstraction, consistency, and information reign supreme. As academics we are dedicated to the categorization, possession, manipulation, and dissemination of information and concepts. While we may undertake important research and teach effectively, our human realm hopes, fears, and desires are supported more than our growth and authenticity are. We are encouraged to devote our time, energy, and mental resources to the ever finer investigation of details of phenomena and concepts. These endeavors usually have limited relevance to daily life and diminish our powers of mind by focusing on narrowly-defined concerns.

Our methodologies in the pursuit of truth are constrained by standards of material measurement and validation and external verification. This stifles our inner explorations and removes discovery and learning from the domain of inner experience. Our capacity for analysis and criticism is not used to lead us in new directions but to enforce a kind of conformity of thinking. Our professional security depends on internalizing the agreed-upon conceptual frameworks of our field and specializing in a small arena over which we can claim expertise and ownership.

As we identify ourselves with our efforts in this ever smaller field of investigation, it appears that we have increasing control over our subject and thereby our world. In fact, our world has shrunk and the unknown can seem even more intimidating.

The material criteria for analysis, verification, and explanation in the scientific and academic communities is particularly troublesome when applied to other domains, such as the aesthetic or the spiritual. If we try to examine Michelangelo's frescoes in the Sistine Chapel with a microscope and calipers, we might conclude that it is made up of various pigments and construction materials with specific atomic structures. We miss what is essential and are blind to the Chapel's beauty, significance and message. If we examine life exclusively in terms of chemistry, electronic impulses, and systems of physical energy or information exchange, we ignore all the non-material factors that sustain life and make up who we are.

Preconceiving Our Relationships

The world of academe is not the only place in which explanations and agreement are valued. When we put such value on understanding, we attribute great significance to explanations in our interactions with others. We want to be understood by other people. We will provide them with elaborate descriptions of our behaviors to get their agreement and support.

When we relate from our human realm heart posture of needing to control life through concepts and understanding, we interact with other people through the filters of what we think we know about them and our own goals for their behavior. We do not really know who they are at the time. Our concepts govern what we hear, how we react, and what we say. We even have concepts about the "relationship" that define it in our minds.

In addition, we try to plan and control our relationships, and thereby social realities and understandings, by making agreements. We use cultural norms (informal agreements) to govern our ideas about reality, behavior and consequences, as well as to form contracts and laws to secure our mutual understandings. This enables us to establish social order and coordinate efforts to meet both individual and community needs. The danger arises when we think that these agreements contain statements of inherent truth and are not subject to doubt or evaluation.

Playing Different Parts

We develop great flexibility of mind in this realm. Our imagination, interests, and concepts lead us in many directions, through all the other realms, and into many circumstances, both real and fantasized. We try to enter the world of other people mentally and identify with them in order to understand what it would be like for us to be in their shoes. We often feel the reality of other people in this way.

However, if we are preoccupied with our fears and our desire for control, we reduce what we learn to information that can be used in deciding what role we must play. As we shift from situation to situation, from person to person, and from goal to goal, we adopt different personae, becoming more attached to our roles than to who we really are.

> All the world's a stage,
> And all the men and women merely players.
> They have their exits and their entrances;
> And one man in his time plays many parts.
>
> *As You Like It, William Shakespeare*

Deciding What We Want

As humans we think about pains and pleasures and we strategize to avoid the first and secure the second. We are constantly comparing and discriminating between options to arrive at precisely what we want. We feel that, if we can be precise enough, we will achieve real satisfaction.

In this realm we are not only concerned with what we "need," as are the pretas, but also with what we desire. Our quest grows from our passion to possess life as a way to feel real, rather than only as a way to fill an inner void. Survival and justice are not enough; pursuing, plotting to attain and realizing the dreams of the mind are that activities that give life meaning and purpose.

We seek to develop an identity based on our dreams and our life-style choices. As our conceptual identity is refined over time, we become fussier, wanting only those things that fit our style, our cultivated self-image. We seek role models so that we can learn how to act, feel, and think from them and thereby be their equals.

We want to be equal to our ideals. We endeavor to create a match between what we want to be and what we are. So our conceptual ideals become guides for action, for developing life plans, and for living day to day.

By relating to concepts that do not exist, we do not actually relate to life. We place concepts, images, explanations, fantasies, and strategies between us and direct experience. Further, once these are cherished, they lead us into the fixations of the other realms and are held in place by the preoccupations, feelings, and habits associated with those realms.

Developing Interests and Avoiding Boredom

Of all the realms, the human realm is most involved with fascination. We are enchanted (one of the meanings of fascination is "enchantment") by our images and our ideals, by our knowledge and our concepts, and by our interests. When we have not yet achieved understanding and are not overwhelmed by confusion, we are in a state of "interest." By being interested in something we select it as a subject for exploration and an object of potential understanding, and thus for a kind of ownership. Interest provides a guide for attention and stimulation. The absence of interest, or boredom, is both extremely uncomfortable and to be avoided.

To avoid boredom, we are constantly searching for new possibilities, new situations, and new ways of improving things. Our dissatisfaction often colors and diminishes our joy. It masks experience of the present with our ambitions for the future. We only notice our present as a step toward making our future better.

Seeking Wholeness through Fragmentation

One double-bind of the human realm is that we try to belong, to be "a part of life," by methodically taking it apart. We want to possess experience by analytical explanation, which breaks it down and separates its components. This fragments us and alienates us from the process of experiencing. In our mental attempts to grasp experience, we are left with only reflections and reconstructions, which are not the experiences themselves. This further cuts us off from the experience of the present moment and from any sense of being genuine.

In another self-defeating behavior, we place conditions on our integrity, postponing our instincts to act virtuously. "Once I have enough money, then I will be generous." "If I meet someone whom I love and who loves me, then I will be loving and feel like being kind." "If I can be sure I will be liked, then I'll take the risk of becoming intimate." These are all forms of conceptual conditions in which we hold our desired actions hostage to preconditions. Each of these conditions results from some insecurity or vanity that we feel must be addressed before we can afford to behave with integrity, to be true to our deeper sense of ourselves. This adds to our inner alienation and fragmentation.

Blinded by Pride

We have difficulty seeing how this occurs because we are also blinded by pride. Cleverness is the pride of this realm. We marvel at how precisely we analyzed situations, constructed plans and strategies, and figured out what things mean. We think we have beat the system, patting ourselves on the back like someone who buys a poster depicting his dream vacation and boasts about what a good deal he got.

We use our cleverness to try to avoid life's cycles, seasons, and stages of growth. We try to maintain our highs through mental manipulations and fantasies, to control physical discomfort through fabricated environments and pain killers, to prevent aging through elixirs and surgery, and to deny death by institutionalizing the dying. We display our knowledge and accomplishments as merit badges for having seized life's secrets and overcome its obstacles.

Masquerading as Philosophers

In our spiritual quest, we search for truth in our conceptual understanding. As rigorous philosophers seeking to know the nature of reality, we create elaborate systems of dialectical analysis and proof to arrive at a place of certainty, where we can be free of doubt. Fleeing our inability to find meaning in our everyday lives, we weave entrancing stories of suffering, struggle, and transformation. We want to remove doubt through images and ideas that feel good and strike us as being right. Instead of wondering about all that we don't know and that cannot be known, we are occupied with what we do know and we want other people to acknowledge how knowledgeable we are. We hesitate to find truth in direct experience, fearing the ways in which we can be deceived by ourselves and other people. We think that awareness is centered in the brain, and exclude the possibility that the mind might be centered in the heart chakra and include the entire body. We enjoy the simplicity of aphorisms, avoiding the work that is required for authentic embodiment of spiritual virtues.

Entering the Other Realms

As Chogyam Trungpa points out, we may have so much going on in our minds from the information we have collected and the plans we have made that we get "stuck in a huge traffic jam of discursive thought." All the planning, all the effort, all the cleverness makes us vulnerable to the other realms. If we succeed at times, we may become gods. If we come close to success when others appear to be successful, we may enter the titan realm. If we feel needy and frustrated, we join the pretas. If we become depressed and feel victimized, we fall into hell. And if we see threats to our efforts, we protect our territory of understanding and plans like the inhabitants of the animal realm.

Like the gods, we can sink into despair and the hells of disillusionment. In the human realm we are led there by our failures and our self-doubts. We may feel like Macbeth when he realizes that all his plots for becoming king have failed:

Out, out, brief candle!
Life's but a walking shadow, a poor player
That struts and frets his hour upon the stage,
And then is heard no more; it is a tale
Told by an idiot, full of sound and fury,
Signifying nothing.

Macbeth, William Shakespeare

Macbeth expounds the deepest fear of the human realm—
the fear that our effort will amount to nothing.

Our desire to be significant and to understand is not only
undermined by events, but by doubt as well. When we doubt
our self-worth, confidence can be destroyed and our esteem
lowered. However, we can also use doubt as a tool to create a
pause in our realm routines.

The Pause That Reflects

The capacity to pause and reflect is the key to interrupting
the habitual patterns of mind in all the realms. It creates a space
in which we can view and question what we are doing and the
ways in which we create suffering. This pause also gives us a
breather from the "busy-ness" of asserting our identities and
our compelling quests. Reflecting on "what is" begins the
process of inquiry and exploration. Gradually, we peel away
the layers of concepts and constructs that obscure our basic
nature and obstruct our aliveness.

Our mind is an essential tool for embarking on the spiritual
path, and the human realm leads most readily into that path
because of its tendency to doubt and create pause. Mind is the
medium for developing meditation, with meditation being a
process for working with whatever frame of mind we are
experiencing.

Breaking Habits and Guiding Growth

While intellectual understanding is not the goal of spiritual work, it provides us with the capacity to change our viewpoints, learn new approaches, and guide our efforts over time. In the human realm, we open our frames of perception and investigate reality to know precisely where we are and what is happening. But we can make this process an ongoing part of spiritual development, along with our desire for and dedication to our own and others' growth and freedom.

As we shift perspectives, we also develop a sense of humor. Each realm has its own characteristic way in which we take ourselves seriously. In the human realm we treat our understanding and concepts, especially those about spirituality, with solemnity. A sense of humor involves looking at any activity, situation, or fixation from a larger perspective and joyfully seeing the irony and humor of our efforts. This does not mean we should turn everything into something funny, for that would crystallize humor into a rule and make it serious. Rather it suggests that we bring to each situation a kind of lightness and joy that is open and flexible.

Chogyam Trungpa tells of a monk who decided to live in a cave and meditate all the time.

> Prior to this he had been thinking continually of pain and suffering. His name was Ngonagpa of Langru, the Black-faced One of Langru, because he never smiled at all but saw everything in life in terms of pain. He remained in retreat for many years, very solemn and deadly honest, until one day he looked at the shrine and saw that someone had presented a big lump of turquoise as a gift to him. As he viewed the gift, he saw a mouse creep in and try to drag away the piece of turquoise. The mouse could not do it, so it went back to its hole and called another mouse. They both tried to drag away this big lump of turquoise but could not do

it. So they squeaked together and called eight more mice who came and finally managed to drag the whole lump back into their hole. Then for the first time Ngonagpa of Langru began to laugh and smile. And that was his first introduction to openness, a sudden flash of enlightenment.

Direct Experience

As we use the space of the pause, our sense of humor, and the tool of inquiry to develop openness, we release the hold of our thinking and simply experience the moment. We are present with this direct experience and this develops our *presence* without the distortions of our concepts and self-images. In the human realm, we have sought to assert and secure our expected presence over time—we would continue to show up. Fearing that forces beyond our control are threats to our continued presence, we have been trying to capture experience and preserve it by freezing it in concepts and memories. Holding on to these mental constructs cuts us off from the direct experience of each living moment.

Being open to what is happening right now—including what is happening in ourselves—without needing to change it is the presence that welcomes direct experience. When we meet a baby, we experience this presence in the baby and ourselves, because the baby is completely in the moment. Similarly, when we listen intently, but without intent, to the field of sound that is coming to us right now, without trying to recognize individual sounds in it, we practice being open to the moment.

Presencing

As we reclaim our natural ability to be open, we directly experience each moment. We realize that we are not simply present, but are *presencing* moment to moment. This *presencing* is the Essence expressing itself through us, and through everything else simultaneously, moment to moment. As we relax into simply being who we are and experiencing this *presencing*, a different understanding opens up to us, which comes from realization rather than thinking. We experience the ease we sought in the human realm when we mistakenly tried to own experience. We have a sense of belonging, not to some thing, some place or some group, but simply to life.

> Mists swirl and dance
> across, around
> the glassy hot pool
>
> Bubbles explode at the surface
> as they meet the sky,
> sending rippling rings to the edges of the universe
>
> Sun radiates, breezes caress, river chants,
> and the heart rests in all that is,
> having found its original home.
>
> *Martin Lowenthal*

Wisdom of Equality

We develop the wisdom of equality, which appreciates the unique value that each of us is and that each of us contributes. We value all things in their uniqueness, knowing that everything is the same in being inherently empty and that each thing is a relative expression of Essence in a unique way. Each moment, each activity, and each person is treated as precious in itself. We realize that each one is best—best at being itself, simply because it is.

When we value everything in this way, we act with enthusiasm and commitment. We love what we are doing. We are totally present. In our absorption, we experience time directly as flow and as a vital energy. The doing is all that is taking place. There is no commentary, no criticism, no distraction of the mind, only presencing as doing. We recognize that each moment is this presencing of awareness.

Generosity of Presence

We manifest our inherent generosity by giving our presence totally to each person, to each situation. Our presence radiates compassion to all. We manifest the three jewels of contribution, participation, and aim, making these accessible to others by our example and by setting the stage for these jewels to arise in them.

Through the equanimity of our presence we treat each person as if he or she were our own child, conveying all the aspects of wisdom to them. We utilize our ability to identify with others, not through the mind of illusion, but through our wisdom mind. We perceive both suffering and wisdom, pain as well as the origins of pain, the burden of habits as well as the ease of freedom. We marvel at the radiance of others, appreciating and encouraging them to be naturally who they are. This is the quality of love, unfettered by attachment and conditions.

In this way we move beyond our self-centered world to extend compassion to all beings. From our hearts, love and compassion radiate like sunlight, shining on all people equally, without exception. This radiance makes no judgments about who people are. We realize the nature that we all share and the Essence from which we all come, from which we derive sustenance, and to which we return.

Clear Mind Meditation

The three meditations suggested here are designed to access the space in awareness beyond thought. The first meditation, used by Zen Master Seung Sahn, involves concentrating the mind by internally repeating two phrases: "clear mind" on the inhalation and "don't know" on the exhalation. Begin, as in other meditations, by placing your attention on either your palm or breath, letting your body and mind ease into the process until you feel relaxed and alert. If you want, expand the inner smile throughout your body. Being in touch with your purpose and desire to become free through your meditation, reflect on the benefits that will come to you and others from this process.

Repeat the phrases "clear mind" and "don't know" to yourself on each inhalation and exhalation. When thoughts arise, watch them. As thoughts about the meaning of these two phrases come to mind, simply note them. You can place your attention in your heart center rather than your head and feel the witnessing awareness of that center. By watching your thoughts carefully enough, you learn to directly experience each thought as it arises and to make contact with the energy within each thought.

When you are very alert and attentive, you may become aware of the space between individual thoughts and between inhalation and exhalation (holding the breath does not count). This is not easy because thoughts quickly slip from one into the next. However, if we relax into the rhythm, we see a "gap" or "space" between thoughts. This space has the quality of openness and presence.

Ajikan

The second meditation uses the sound AH. This exercise is adapted from a Tibetan Dzogchen practice and the Japanese tantric practice of Ajikan. AH is considered the primal sound of the universe from which all other sounds, speech, and language derive. Its vibration penetrates all things. The sound made when the mouth first opens is the sound AH.

This exercise consists of the repetition of AH aloud four times and listening silently to the AH of the universe on what would be the fifth time. Each repetition is done with a breath, saying the syllable on the exhalation. During each spoken repetition, visualize an ever-encompassing radiant ball of light.

Pronounce AH the first time, feeling the sensation of the sound, and visualize the radiant ball of light expanding from an infinitesimally small point in the core of the heart until it fills the chest cavity.

Continuing to attend to sensations, pronounce the second AH, expanding the radiant ball of light until it fills the space surrounding the body—a little more than an arm's length.

Attending to the sensations, pronounce the third AH, expanding the radiant ball of light until it includes the entire universe as far as you can imagine.

Continuing to attend to sensations, pronounce the fourth AH, imagining that the radiant ball of light continues to expand into the unknown beyond your imagination.

Finally, abide and listen with your whole being to the space of space and to the vibration from which all sound arises.

This can be done as many times as feels comfortable. Close your meditation by dedicating the positive energy you have generated to the freedom and happiness of all beings.

Welcoming Presence

The third meditation is similar to the first one in this chapter. The difference is that instead of using the phrases of that meditation, on the inhalation you say to yourself "welcoming" and on the exhalation you say "presence." If you are quiet enough, you can coordinate the "welcoming" and the "presence" with the rhythms of your heart beat. As you do this, feel yourself being here and sense the mystery of your own existence.

As we open our hearts and release the hold of concepts, we feel the borders of our contracted world dissolve. We experience with our entire being and not simply with our head. Everything feels immediate and rich, and we are fully engaged in all our interactions. Because there are no conditions to our presence, other people feel more supported in being themsel-

ves. Then the loving reciprocity of our mutual presencing reveals the hidden communion beyond our thoughts of separation and feelings of aloneness.

PART III

*The Practice of Compassion
and the Fruit of Freedom*

10

Meditating to Embody Compassion

It is no use walking anywhere to preach unless our
walking is our preaching.

St. Francis of Assisi

I take upon myself the burden of all suffering.
I am determined to bear it.
I shall not turn back.
I shall not flee or tremble.
I shall not yield or hesitate.
Why? Because the liberation of all beings is my vow.

Shantideva

COMPASSION GROWS from our instinct to help others.
Approaching life with compassion leads to wisdom and
is itself developed with wisdom. With insight into the nature
of suffering and how it arises, we liberate our dynamics of
aliveness from our realm preoccupations. We acquire the wisdom to accept our limitations and to do what we can, not
worrying about what we cannot do.

What is important is our attitude of compassion; it is of no
use to think that we can actually eliminate someone elses pain
while our own mind is still troubled. Our goal is to continue
to work on the development of the wisdom of clarity at the
same time that we cultivate the compassionate wish to alleviate
the suffering of others. Eventually we want to embody com-

passion as an active way of relating to others, with the heart posture of being a beneficial presence.

By entering into a spiritual relationship with Avalokiteshvara, the embodiment of compassion, we awaken and develop our own potential for compassion. We build this spiritual relationship by practicing an ancient and powerful meditation that involves visualizing ourselves as the Great Compassionate One, contemplating the underlying dynamics and wisdoms of the realms, and reciting Avalokiteshvara's mantra.

This mantra, *OM MANI PADME HUM,* expresses the energy of compassion that we all possess. By repeating the mantra, we focus our mind on the qualities of aliveness, wisdom, and compassion associated with the figure of Avalokiteshvara. A mantra, as a series of syllables, also corresponds to certain subtle vibrations within us. Its effectiveness is realized in our experience of its sound as we say it aloud or silently.

By using a mantra we activate energies within us and awaken the awareness and wisdom qualities that are associated with it. We can say mantras either during meditation or while going about our daily activities. By concentrating on the compassion-mantra, our mind also remains alert and dedicated rather than tired and troubled.

As we work at a deeper level, we realize that Avalokiteshvara is compassion and is therefore available within all of us, needing only to be actualized. In this practice we identify as the Great Compassionate One. We use the syllables of the mantra to enter each of the six realms of suffering, and imagine boundless radiance shining from our heart center and illuminating all beings caught in that world of pain. In this way, we extend our practice into every domain of life, moving beyond our self-concerns, and we integrate our spiritual work into the world in which we live.

Radiating to the Worlds of Pain

Begin by directing your attention to your desire to be of benefit to all beings by reciting an aspiration prayer such as the following:

Aspiration Vows of Awakening Being

May I attain as quickly as possible the liberating transcendence that awakens the highest expression of Essence and radiates beneficial presence to all.

Though the means to awakening are beyond number, may I master them all.

Though the causal seeds of suffering seem endless, may I burn them all in radiant presence.

Though beings are beyond count and imagination, may I serve to liberate them all.

Then place your attention on your palm or breath, letting your body and mind ease into the process until you feel relaxed and alert. Expand the inner smile throughout your body. Being in touch with your purpose and desire to become free through your meditation, sense the benefits that will come to you and others from this process.

Imagine yourself as Avalokiteshvara, as a manifestation of pure unobstructed compassion, love and wisdom. Your body is radiant, composed of transparent white light. Your smiling face radiates peace and love. You have a thousand arms with an eye in the palm of each one. With nine heads, you look out in all directions.

In your heart center imagine a wheel that is divided into six parts with a radiating crystal in the center. Each part represents the dynamic and wisdom qualities of a different realm, has a radiant color, and corresponds to a syllable of the mantra. In the front center section is the dynamic of wonderment and the wisdom of gratitude and of Essence. The color is white and the corresponding syllable is *OM*. The section in the front right is the dynamic of harmony and the wisdom of skillful means, with the color emerald green and the syllable *MA*. The front left section is the dynamic of direct experience and presence and the wisdom of equality, with the color brilliant yellow and the syllable *NI*. The back left section is the dynamic of relating and the wisdom of spaciousness, with the color of blue and the syllable *PA*. The section at the back right is the dynamic of value generation and the wisdom of radiance and generosity, with the color ruby red and the syllable *DME*. The section at the center back is the dynamic of flow, the quality of patience, and the mirror-like wisdom of emptiness, with the color indigo or purple and the syllable *HUM*.

All space around you, beyond even the horizon, is filled with beings. Consider their suffering. Begin by considering the suffering of the god realm and, with your inhalation, draw that suffering as a dull white color into the front center section of your heart chakra and into the crystal at the very center of your heart. Holding your breath, sense that suffering breaking down into its most elemental dynamic energy. Then, on your exhalation, saying *OM*, radiate the dynamic of wonderment, the wisdom of gratitude, and the color white to your parents, your loved ones, to all the people you know, and finally to all beings without exception.

Repeat this process with each of the other five dynamics and their corresponding realms.

Realm	Color	Section of Heart	Syllable	Dynamic	Color
god	dull white	front center	OM	wonderment	white
titan	burnt red	front right	MA	harmony	green
human	dull blue	front left	NI	direct experience	yellow
animal	dull green	back left	PA	relating	blue
preta	dull yellow	back right	DME	value generation	red
hell	smokey grey	back center	HUM	flow, patience	indigo

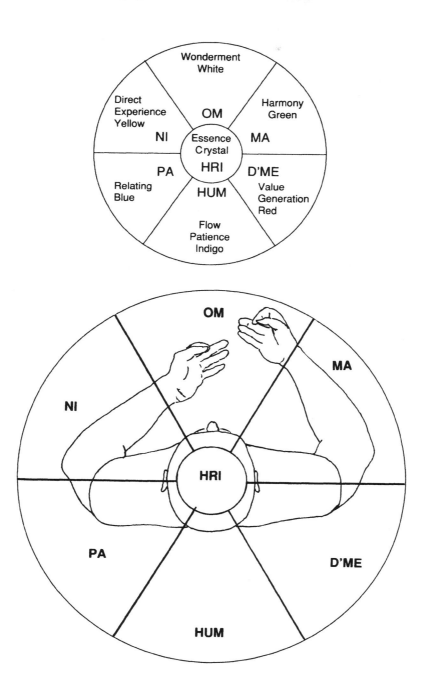

Remember that suffering, unhappiness and pain are impermanent mental experiences that arise from misunderstanding and confusion. Recall your clarity. So, as you open your heart and radiate the qualities, feel how wonderful it would be if everyone were free.

Silently radiate the crystal clear light of Essence and the syllable HRI in the pause at the end of the mantra. Having completed this cycle once slowly, repeat the mantra and radiate from each part of your heart center as before. Do this as many times as feels comfortable. A full set of repetitions is usually 108.

You will be most successful with this meditation when you remain relaxed and comfortable, feeling every cell in your body radiating the energy of compassion. It is said that one recitation of the mantra with full awareness can result in enlightenment and is worth thousands of repetitions that are done mechanically.

When you have completed your recitation and visualization, release any effort and abide. Finally, dedicate the energy from your meditation to the freedom and happiness of all living beings using the "Four Immeasurable Thoughts."

> May all beings have happiness and that which produces happiness.
>
> May all beings be free from suffering and that which produces suffering.
>
> May all beings be established in the inherent joy that transcends suffering.
>
> May all beings abide in equanimity, free from ignoring, grabbing, and fighting, which form the tyranny of like and dislike.

11

Awakening to Aliveness and the Realization of Freedom

The century since Franz Kafka was born has been marked by the idea of "modernism"—a self-consciousness new among centuries, a consciousness of being new. Kafka epitomizes one aspect of the modern mind-set: a sensation of anxiety and shame whose center cannot be located and therefore cannot be placated; a sense of an infinite difficulty within things, impeding every step; a sensitivity acute beyond usefulness, as if the nervous system, flayed of its old hide of social usage and religious belief, must record every touch as pain.

John Updike

I believe that at every level of society—familial, tribal, national and international—the key to a happier and more successful world is the growth of compassion. We do not need to become religious, nor do we need to believe in an ideology. All that is necessary is for each of us to develop our good human qualities. I try to treat whoever I meet as an old friend. This gives me a genuine feeling of happiness. It is the practice of compassion.

Tenzin Gyatso, the Fourteenth Dalai Lama

IN MODERN MATERIAL CULTURES, our uncertainty in the face of intimacy and pain makes us particularly vulnerable to the fears, desires, and ignorance that generate suffering. While our cultural attitudes toward pain may be evolving, the nature of suffering and its centrality to the human condition have not changed. Suffering is part of the process of growth, and its transcendence is dependent upon our continuing that growth. Our design as human beings, and the nature of all reality, lead to a gradual awakening if we open to our natural aliveness and freedom.

As this book has suggested and our own experience can verify, we have the capacity to interrupt our habitual patterns of mind and body and to tap an awareness that goes beyond the necessities of our material lives and the limitations of our assumptions. As our investigation into the realms brings familiarity and insight, our own basic nature and the nature of the universe are revealed.

Opening to Other People

Opening to other people is critical to our growth and happiness, as well as to the well-being of our community. Our emotional patterns arise and are played out daily in relation to others. To remove the process of discovery of aliveness from the social context of our lives is like trying to explore the beauty of an image by investigating a single dot. The idea is not to withdraw from the whole, but to realize the context of the whole through us.

We often see ourselves in other people more readily than we do when we are alone. If we work only for our own liberation from suffering, we are unlikely to gain such self-knowledge. On the other hand, if we work to relieve the suffering of other people, then our own comes into perspective and our inner world opens from the closed system of self-preoccupation.

Cultivating Wonder through Intimacy

Through closeness and intimacy with other people, we cultivate wonder at the variety of expressions of Essence, and develop fearlessness toward the unknown. Intimacy also creates the possibility of overcoming the assumption of a separate self, alienated and distant from others. When we cultivate intimacy in relation to all people, including our enemies, we become free of the tension of being alienated from any manifestation of the divine.

Expanding Our Love

Our capacity for love is extended and expanded as we relate to our own suffering and that of others. We understand our interdependence, our shared desire for connection and belonging, and our common nature. We see the opportunities for love and freedom that await each of us when we awaken to that nature. Through our realization of radiance, we see and receive the radiance of others, no matter what their condition, and radiate our own presence to them.

As we realize the preciousness of human life and notice the ways in which our life is sustained by other people, our love and gratitude deepen our experience of belonging. We welcome the opportunities to share and enthusiastically participate and contribute as we express our uncontrived compassion.

Developing Our Compassion

Compassion begins with our ability to reflect and pause in our unconscious behaviors and to follow our instinct to help others. By exploring the realms of pain, we then explore both the nature of our suffering and that of others. Our capacity to identify with those worlds permits us to get inside them. We discover how the realms are constructed as contexts of pain. We see how, in each realm, we feel compelled to prove something about ourselves. As we deepen the process of exploration, we awaken the awareness that has always been there and within which all experience arises.

As we come to realize this essential aspect of our being, an all-penetrating force of compassion radiates from us. This compassion is open, free, and without boundaries. Although we cannot describe it or comprehend it intellectually, we can observe it. We manifest it in our spaciousness of being, our spontaneous responses, the value we create, our freshness, skillfulness, and harmony of action, our appreciation and wonder, and the presence that we generously offer to all.

Everything Arises within Awareness

Awareness is not something outside of our experience, nor is it a product of our experience. We realize that, not only is the world of experience a product of awareness, but so, too, is all reality. This universal, transcendent awareness is realized only after we have opened to, explored, and come to know the basic nature of the mind and its power. The true awakening or recognition of this nature is called "enlightenment."

Transcendent awareness does not mean an awareness that is removed from or beyond the material world. "Transcendent" refers to that which is beyond all concepts; it transcends all categories of thought and all notions of time, space, and knowledge.

Cultivating Transcendent Awareness

With the proper use of our mind, we transcend our conceptual inclinations by creating a pause. Then, as we open the boundaries of our mental territories, we engage in the process of learning, and through our spaciousness we include the unknown into our awareness. As we release our feelings of victimization and our anger, we develop patience with the ever-changing situations of life, observing the flow and realizing that awareness itself is *becoming*. Going beyond our own neediness, we instinctively become aware of the radiance of life and we contribute our radiance to others. In addition, when we relax from the quest for power and the competition to prove our worth, our capacity for fresh, harmonious action arises. In our successes, avoiding the seduction of comfort and conceit, we awaken to the sense of wonder, to the recognition of change, relationship, and emptiness, and to the deeper opening of the heart that comes from gratitude and appreciation. Being authentically present, our experience is direct and our natural enthusiasm manifests in all our actions.

Awareness is the only ground of our experience. Every aspect of our life occurs within awareness with perfect equanimity. Experience is the image in the mirror-like surface of awareness. If we pay exclusive attention to images and ignore the mirror, we lose sight of the context from which they arise. Just as the image is inseparable from the mirror, so, too, is awareness wedded to everyday experience. All images and concepts are themselves manifestations within awareness.

Luminosity of Awareness

Awareness is luminous. It reveals anything and everything, even in the dark. We see this brilliance in our dreams, even though our eyes are closed and no apparent physical light exists inside our head. This luminous energy can transform the frozen energy of any fixation or emotion into awareness itself, just as sunlight melts ice into water, heats the water into vapor, and the vapor expands into space.

Realizing Our Freedom

When we awaken, the "we" disappears as a reference for understanding and realization. This is not to say there is no personality or ego, for these are part of our manifestation and functioning in the world. Rather, presuming a position from which to understand anything is regarded as a mere vanity. Everything exists simultaneously everywhere as complete openness. This cannot be grasped by our senses or encompassed in our concepts, yet these senses and concepts are included within the nature of reality. Our freedom is *from* the vanity of position and *to* the expression of aliveness.

When we understand that the foundation of freedom and aliveness is not any concept, any place, or any condition other than what is, we will realize that we have always been free and alive. We know that our being and becoming arise out of, are permeated by, and are none other than awakened awareness, just as a color arises from light and a note of music is a part of sound. Essence is. All there is is *is*.

When we experience being free, we live authentically without reactive resistance, the tension of alienation, the inhibition of doubt, and the agenda of validation. We are open and responsive to all aspects of experience. We participate fully in life and contribute our aliveness to every situation freely. Our confidence comes from being true to ourselves and the nature of life.

Serving the World as Spiritual Practice

Spiritual practice does not require that we leave the world. In fact, properly viewed, it expands our vision beyond our self-centered concerns to a more spontaneous whole. Our openness to others, their suffering, and their role in our own growth leads naturally to sharing and service.

In this adventure of growth and service, we confront many subtle forms of our preconceptions and old habits. As Jack Kornfield points out, love, compassion, and equanimity must be distinguished from their "near-enemies." The near-enemy of love is attachment, entangling us in desire rather than allowing us to relate with appreciation and honor. The near-enemy of compassion is pity, which separates us from others instead of expressing our shared nature. The near-enemy of equanimity is indifference, which manifests as withdrawal rather than as unperturbable engagement in the world.

How much of our time and energy is devoted to formal practice and how much to service will depend on our level of development, what we need to cultivate, and the conditions and needs of ourselves and those around us. With time, every activity becomes a meditation, and the distinctions between practice and everyday life dissolve. Prior to that, there are no prescriptions for a "correct" balance. The proportions will vary during different periods in life. In each situation we can ask what is needed, not for ourselves alone, but for other people and the situation as a whole. The key is to perceive the Divine or Essence in each person and in each moment, and to dedicate our presence and our activities to sharing that realization so that others may experience the joy of freedom.

Being a Warrior of Compassion

The forces of fixation and pain seem so pervasive in our world that we may feel confused about where we should start and how much we can do. This is the time to take a stance as a warrior of compassion. As warriors, our dedication and passion protect us from being intimidated and overwhelmed. Our skill directs us toward getting results. Our committed action keeps us present without the interference of self-doubt. Our open wonder maintains the joy of the effort and the gratitude for the opportunity. Our spaciousness keeps us connected and protects us from the alienation of separation. Our knowledge of emptiness maintains our ability to avoid righteousness, to flow with the process with patience, to have humor, and to engage fully. And our generosity of spirit radiates to all without the need for acknowledgment or credit. As warriors, our deep inner urge to help others is not obscured by fear and self-consciousness, but is embodied as a path. Our actions free others while manifesting our own freedom to be naturally who we are.

May This Work Truly Serve
And Only Be Of Benefit To All

Bibliography

Blofeld, John E.C. *Bodhisattva of Compassion: The Mystical Tradition of Kuan Yin.* Boston: Shambhala, 1977.

Bly, Robert. *Iron John.* Reading: Addison-Wesley, 1990.

Buddha, Shakyamuni. "Anguttara-Nikaya," in *World Of the Buddha: A Reader.* Edited and with Introduction and Commentaries by Lucien Stryk. Garden City: Doubleday Anchor, 1969.

Campbell, Joseph. *The Inner Reaches of Outer Space: Metaphor As Myth and As Religion.* New York: Alfred van der Marck, 1985.

Campbell, Joseph, with Bill Moyers. *The Power of Myth.* Edited by Betty Sue Flowers. New York: Doubleday, 1988.

Chogyam, Ngakpa. *Journey Into Vastness: A Handbook of Tibetan Meditation Techniques.* Longmead: Element Books, 1988.

Einstein, Albert. "What I Believe," in *The Forum.* October, 1930.

Eliot, T.S. *The Cocktail Party, A Comedy.* New York: Harcourt Brace, 1950.

___. "Burnt Norton," in *Collected Poems, 1909-1962.* New York: Harcourt, Brace & World, 1963.

Fields, Rick. "The Changing of the Guard: Western Buddhism in the Eighties." Tricycle: The Buddhist Review, Winter 1991.

Frost, Robert. "Two Tramps in Mud Time," in *Collected Poems of Robert Frost.* Garden City: Halcyon House, 1942.

Gyatso, Tenzin, The Fourteenth Dalai Lama. *Compassion and the Individual.* Boston: Wisdom Publications, 1991.

191

Gibran, Kahlil. *The Prophet.* New York: Knopf, 1952.

Goldstein, Joseph, and Jack Kornfield. *Seeking the Heart of Wisdom: The Path of Insight Meditation.* Boston: Shambhala, 1987.

Goleman, Daniel. *Vital Lies, Simple Truths.* New York: Simon & Schuster, 1985.

Govinda, Lama Anagarika. *Foundations of Tibetan Mysticism.* York Beach: Samuel Weiser, 1969.

__. *Creative Meditation and Multi-Dimensional Consciousness.* Wheaton: Quest Books, 1976.

Hanh, Thich Nhat. *Interbeing, Commentaries on the Tiep Hien Precepts.* Berkeley: Parallax Press, 1987.

Heller, Joseph. *Catch-22.* New York: Simon & Schuster, 1961.

Kahn, Hazrat Inayat. *Complete Sayings of Hazrat Inayat Kahn.* New York: Omega Publications, 1978.

LeGuin, Ursula. *Lathe of Heaven.* New York: Avon, 1973.

Lao Tsu. *The Way of Life: According to Laotzu.* Translated by Witter Bynner. New York: Perigee, 1980.

Mann, John and Lar Short. *The Body of Light: History and Practical Techniques for Awakening Your Subtle Body.* New York: Globe Press Books, 1990.

McDonald, Kathleen. *How to Meditate: A Practical Guide.* Edited by Robina Courtin. London: Wisdom Publications, 1984.

Milne, A.A. *Winnie the Pooh.* New York: Dell, 1954.

Rabten, Geshe. *Song of the Profound View.* London: Wisdom Publications, 1989.

Sahn, Zen Master Seung. *Dropping Ashes on the Buddha: The Teachings of Zen Master Seung Sahn.* Compiled and edited by Stephen Mitchell. New York: Grove Press, 1976.

__. *Only Don't Know: The Teachings Letters of Zen Master Seung Sahn.* San Francisco: Four Seasons, 1982.

Saint Francis of Assisi. *The Little Flowers of St. Francis.* Translated by Raphael Brown. Garden City: Image Books, 1958.

Santayana, G. *Life of Reason.* New York: Dover, 1982.

Sartre, Jean Paul. "Huis Clos," *No Exit, and Three Other Plays.* Translated by L. Abel. New York: Vintage, 1976.

Senzaki, Nyogen. *Like a Dream, Like a Fantasy.* Edited by Eido Shimano Roshi. Tokyo: Japan Publications, 1978.

Shakespeare, William. *As You Like It.* New Haven: Yale University Press, 1954.

___. *Julius Caesar.* New Haven: Yale University Press, 1919.

___. *Macbeth.* New Haven: Yale University Press, 1954.

Short, Lar. *Dying to Go Beyond.* Albuquerque: Grace Essence Fellowship, 1992.

___. *The Way of Radiance.* Durango: We Are Publishing, 1986.

Sogyal Rinpoche. *Dzogchen and Padmasambhava.* Berkeley: Rigpa Fellowship, 1990.

Thoreau, Henry David. *Walden, or, Life in the Woods.* Franklin Center: Franklin Library, 1983.

Thurman, Robert. "Tibet, Its Buddhism and Its Art," in *Wisdom and Compassion: The Sacred Art of Tibet.* New York: Harry Abrams, 1991.

Tolstoy, Leo. "What is Art?" in *What is Art? and Other Essays.* London: Oxford University Press, 1962.

Trungpa Rinpoche, Chogyam. *Cutting Through Spiritual Materialism.* Berkeley: Shambhala, 1973.

Tarthang Tulku. *Hidden Mind of Freedom.* Berkeley: Dharma, 1981.

___. *Openness Mind.* Berkeley: Dharma, 1978.

___. *Skillful Means.* Berkeley: Dharma, 1978.

Updike, John. "Reflections: Kafka's Short Stories." *The New Yorker.* May 9, 1983, 121.

MARTIN LOWENTHAL, Ph.D. is an ordained senior meditation teacher, founder and mentor with the Dedicated Life Institute. Dr. Lowenthal is the author of *Alchemy of the Soul, Dawning of Clear Light,* and *Embrace Yes*. In addition to creating and teaching trainings, workshops and retreats internationally, he serves as pastoral counselor, consultant, and writer. He has been on the faculty of Boston College and Harvard University Externsion and has studied with Buddhist and Taoist masters for more than thirty years. Dr. Lowenthal received his doctorate from the University of California, Berkeley in 1970, has worked as an applied anthropologist in Botswana, Africa, and directed a research institute from 1970 to 1977.

The Dedicated Life Institute (DLI) supports spiritual exploration and growth and is dedicated to making the essence teachings of many traditions accessible in a Western idiom. Incorporating the principles of the mystic way, we promote both recovery of our wisdom ground of being and development of our capacity to use our daily conditions as a means of growth and the opportunity to manifest our true wisdom nature. Our dedication to living as an expression of wisdom serves to encourage both personal and social transformation. The Institute offers meditation groups, retreats, workshops, and a home study program. For more information please visit our website at www.dli.org, email us at mldli@rcn.org or call us at 617-527-8606.

LAR SHORT, is the Maestro, Spiritual Director, and founder of Grace Essence Fellowship (G.E.F). GEF is a modern Esoteric Work School that is based on the natural human potential for awakening to freedom. As a non-dogmatic, non-sectarian spiritual school, GEF has made valuable teachings available in an open-system format for over 32 years. These teachings include the esoteric work and principles found at the heart of the spiritual traditions of humanity, and builds upon them to produce easily accessible, modern formats.

Lar has created and taught many trainings and retreats, including *Opening the Heart of Compassion* which gave rise to this book. He has also co-authored *Body of Light* with John Mann, which has been translated into 6 languages. Other books by Lar Short include *The Way of Radiance*, *Dying To Go Beyond*, and *Commuter Yoga*.

He is the first to apply accelerated learning techniques to the learning of holistic health practices, and to the learning of spiritual work. He created BodyMind Clearing (a system of body work and trauma release), and the holistic health training format Total Person Facilitation, a synthesis of Eastern and Western approaches. He was a pioneering influence in the Natural Childbirth and Natural Death Care movements. Lar has over 45 years of formal practice and teaching experience in Eastern and Western martial arts, energetic work, internal alchemy, and meditation systems.

Grace Essence Fellowship, P.O. Box 2129, El Prado, NM 87529, LarShort@gmail.com